Got *Lean?*

Discovering the Missing Piece of the Puzzle

Randy Lubbers

Got Lean?

Discovering the Missing Piece of the Puzzle

Copyright © 2009
Randall Lubbers

This book is copyrighted material. All rights are reserved.

It is against the law to make copies of this material without getting specific written permission in advance from Randall Lubbers. No part of this publication may be reproduced, stored in a retrieval system, or transmitted in any form or by any means, electronic, mechanical, photocopying, recording or otherwise, without prior written permission of the author. For information, or for additional copies, please visit our web site at
www.lubbersandassociates.com.

ISBN: 978-0-9639895-4-3

Published in the USA by
WordExcel LLC
Hamilton, MI

Printed in the USA by
Morris Publishing®
3212 East Highway 30
Kearney, NE 68847
1-800-650-7888

How To Use This Book

I have written this book to be a resource for both individuals and small groups. Utilize the following to get the greatest benefit from this book:

- **The text.** The main element of this book is the text. It encompasses many years of experience and practice.
- **The practice exercises.** At the end of each chapter is a practice exercise to assist you in retaining and better understanding what you read.
- **The self assessment.** At the end of each chapter is a self-assessment that allows you to measure the current state, either as an individual, group, department, or organization. It points out areas of strength and weakness from which improvement goals and action plans can be created.
- **The group discussion questions.** At the end of each chapter is a set of group discussion questions that assist any team or group wanting to discuss critical issues that affect performance and competitiveness.

These tools can be used individually or as a group. Of great value might be a brown bag lunch every week for an hour. Each week, each person individually reads the chapter, completes the practice exercise, and fills in the self assessment. Then, in the one hour brown bag lunch session, the group together discusses the group discussion questions, how the assessments were filled out, and creates action plans for improvement.

No matter how you use this book, my desire and wish is that it assists you on your path to excellence and success.

Got Lean?   Table of Contents

Introduction
    My Passion 10
    Thoughts before We Start 11
    The Reason for this Book 14
    My Definition of Lean 18

Overview of the Six Laws of Lean
    The Six Laws of Lean 22
    Law #1: Lean Requires that You take Everyone
            with You. 24
    Law #2: Lean is a Culture 25
    Law #3: Lean Must Encompass Every Area . 26
    Law #4: Lean is a Way of Thinking . . 27
    Law #5: Lean Focuses on Results, Not Activities   28
    Law #6: Lean is a Set of Tools, or Methods, for
            Finding and Eliminating Waste. . 29
    How We Get it Wrong 30

Law #1: Lean Requires that You take Everyone with You
    Law #1: Lean Requires that You take Everyone
          with You 36
    The Barrier 38
    Desire 40
    Creating Desire 42
    Ownership 47
    Conclusion 50
    Practice Exercise: Law #1 52
    Law #1: Self Assessment 55
    Law #1: Group Discussion Questions . . 56
    Practice Exercise Answer Sheet . . . 57

Law #2: Lean is a Culture
    Law #2: Lean is a Culture 60
    Culture Change 62
    Conclusion 77
    Practice Exercise: Law #2. 80
    Law #2: Self Assessment 84
    Law #2: Group Discussion Questions . . 85
    Practice Exercise Answer Sheet . . . 86

Law #3: Lean Must Encompass Every Area

Law #3: Lean Must Encompass Every Area	88
Mistake #1	88
Mistake #2	89
Blur the Lines	93
Perfect Attendance	93
We Must Work Together	95
Mix Them Up	95
It Takes Horsepower	96
Key People May Resist	96
Conclusion	98
Practice Exercise: Law #3	99
Law #3: Self Assessment	102
Law #3: Group Discussion Questions	103
Practice Exercise Answer Sheet	104

Law #4: Lean is a Way of Thinking

Law #4: Lean is a Way of Thinking	106
Why the Need to Change	107
Every Person must Change	107
Thinking in a New Way	108
Patience, Control and Chaos	109
Learn to Think Differently	110
Learn to See Waste	111
Theoretically Perfect Goals	114
Overcome the Obstacles	115
Getting Things Done Takes Horsepower	117
Bribery Works	118
Suggestion Systems Get You in Trouble	119
Be a Professional	121
Continue to Learn	121
We Can't Change Time, But We Can Change How We Use It.	122
Elevate your Constraint.	122
20-50-30 Rule Applied to Technical Skills	123
People must be Self-Managed.	124
Good Judgment	128
Marketing vs. Selling	128
Stop Doing it and See if Anyone Notices	129
Breeding Ground for 30 Percenters.	129
Changing Habits	129
Getting Traction	130

Think "Perfect", not "Good enough" . . 130
Maintenance People Must Change Their Mindset 130
Anticipate What Can Happen. . . . 131
Be Like the Maytag Repairman . . . 131
Technical Approach vs. People Approach . 132
Think Process not People 132
Outrun the "Foot". 133
The Guy Called "They" Doesn't Exist . . 133
Conclusion 134
Practice Exercise: Law #4. 136
Law #4: Self Assessment 140
Law #4: Group Discussion Questions . . 141
Practice Exercise Answer Sheet . . . 142

Law #5: Lean Focuses on Results, Not Activities

Law #5: Lean Focuses on Results, Not Activities 144
Lean Metrics Defined 144
Lean Metrics and Empowerment . . . 145
Greatest Obstacles 148
Scoreboard Obstacles 150
Want to Improve? You Gotta Keep Score! . 153
Measurement, Start to Finish . . . 154
Additional Thoughts 155
Set Goals 156
Process Fixation 159
Helpful Hints on Creating a Scoreboard . . 160
Conclusion 165
Practice Exercise: Law #5. 167
Law #5: Self Assessment 170
Law #5: Group Discussion Questions . . 171
Practice Exercise Answer Sheet . . . 172

Law #6: Lean is a Set of Tools, or Methods, for Finding and Eliminating Waste

Law #6: Lean is a Set of Tools, or Methods,
  For Finding and Eliminating Waste . 174
Build a House with a Hammer? . . . 174
Start Simply. 175
Dancing to the Oldies 176
Why We Fail 177
The Tools of Lean 178
Tool Matrix 179

5S	180
5S – Sort	181
5S – Set in Order	183
5S – Shine	184
5S – Standardize	187
5S – Sustain	188
Kaizen	190
Kaizen Event: Benefits and Drawbacks	191
Value Stream Mapping	193
SMED – Single Minute Exchange of Dies	195
Setup Time Reduction – What's it Worth?	195
Total Productive Maintenance (TPM)	199
Definition (TPM)	199
Goals (TPM)	199
Critical Factors (TPM)	200
Responsibilities within TPM	202
Kanban	204
What is Kanban?	204
The Goals of Kanban	205
Action Plans to Create a Kanban System	205
Pareto Analysis	207
5W's and an H	211
Conclusion	214
Practice Exercise: Law #6	215
Law #6: Self Assessment	220
Law #6: Group Discussion Questions	221
Practice Exercise Answer Sheet	222

Leadership for Sustainability

Leadership for Sustainability	224
Accountability Starts at the Top	236
Grow People Who "Get It"	237
People, Process, and Technology	239
The Boss from Hell	239
It Must Start at The Top?	240
Consistency vs. Flexibility	242
Don't' Back Off or Ease Up	243
Take the Right People With You	244
Stop Placing Blame and Get Moving	245
Where is Your Focus?	246
Situations Will Set You Up	247
Beware The Sabotager?	247

Where Leaders Get It Wrong	250
You Must Lead!	251
The Benefits	252
Conclusion	252
Practice Exercise: Leadership for Sustainability	254
Lean Sustainability Self Assessment	259
Lean Sustainability Group Discussion Questions	260
Practice Exercise Answer Sheet	261

Odd and Ends

Everyone has Different Gifts and Talents	264
Choosing a Trainer or Consultant	265
Do You Need a Lean Champion?	266
Do You Need a Lean Team?	268
What are the Characteristics of a Sustained Lean Process?	269
Why Do Organizations Fail to Sustain Lean?	269
Sequence of Events	270
How to Get Traction	272
Junior High Behavior	273
The Stages of Lean Implementation	274
Have You Discovered the Missing Piece of the Puzzle?	275

Reference Bibliography 276

Index 277

About the Author 283

Other Products and Services. . . . 285

My Passion

I've been in business for 15 years and in that time I've had the privilege of interacting with dozens of organizations, from libraries to those who make castings. My motivation, like most people, is to make a living. My passion, however, is to assist people and organizations become more competitive... to be the best. It's difficult to put into words how to describe it when someone walks up to you, shakes your hand, and says, *"You changed my life. Thank you!"* It's incredibly humbling when someone introduces you to thirty people that make up the management team of their company as *"one of my mentors... the person who changed my life ten years ago."* It blows me away! But it also reminds me... It's not about me. These people did the hard work, not me. I'm the personal trainer, the coach, the mentor. My passion is to help, and each time I see the results, I set the bar higher for myself to be a better coach. Can we do it better, faster, with less pain next time? Are there improved methods that achieve better results faster? I am committed to developing them! I am committed to your success! It's my passion!

Randy Lubbers
September 25, 2009

Thoughts before We Start

- I tell it like it is. I tell you what you need to hear, not what you want to hear... But I will always be respectful. Remember, I'm here to help.
- I know things are never perfect. Even if you follow my advice perfectly, things won't always end up perfectly.
- I'm told on occasion that I make lots of general comments. I realize that. I know that not everything is true in every situation. Each situation is different and unique. You can't, and shouldn't try to apply everything the way someone else has. It's your challenge to apply the concept to your specific situation.
- This book is my attempt at a shameless sales pitch. If you need my help, call me.
- In leading any organization through the Lean journey, I use a specific sequence and activities in which people experience the subject. This book cannot begin to cover this process, but it does explain the theory behind what I do.
- This book is not, and cannot be, a primer on Lean. Not every detail of Lean is included.
- The thoughts and details in each chapter will both overlap and be repeated. I tried to do my best at separating them, but I was more concerned with flow and completing a thought.

- While some of the actions I describe can be implemented on an individual basis, sustainability is assured only if you implement the entire strategy described in this book.
- Some of you may think that my approach seems simplistic. In reality it's incredibly difficult and time consuming to get it right. There are no easy answers. There are no shortcuts. There's no silver bullet and no magic pill! Sorry.
- I have accumulated the thoughts, information, and advice that you find in this book over the course of more than 34 years in and around business and industry. Everything here comes from my own experience. I have not read several books and compiled some of the best stuff that you should try. I know this stuff works because I've used it, made lots of mistakes, and improved it over time. I do not ask you to try something I have not tested.
- My approach to Lean is different compared to others. Most people focus only on the "technical" aspect – the tools. I focus on the entire organization. I'll put my success rate, or rather, the success rate of the organizations I've assisted, up against anyone else. I know this because I follow behind "everyone else". Different works!
- I don't make a big deal out of Lean. If you make a big deal out of it, people will resist it. Lean is

common sense and people have been doing it all of their lives. You are simple challenging them to be more intentional about doing what they've always done! If you treat it like it's new and different, and people have been doing it all of their lives, you will lose credibility. They'll see right through you. So don't make a big deal of it. It's like scoring a touchdown. Act like you've been there before.

- Take the book as a whole. If you have a question as you read through one section, it may be answered in another.

The Reason for this Book

Have you ever put together a jigsaw puzzle where you get right down to the end and the last piece is missing? Drives you crazy doesn't it? You look all over. Under the table and chairs... in everyone's pockets and cuffs. The longer it takes to find, the crazier you get. You start blaming people for hiding it and you get frantic trying to find it. This is what many organizations act like when trying to implement Lean. It's what pops into my head when I listen to their stories.

Almost every company I work with has tried Lean several times. They tell me, *"Randy, we've done Kaizen Events, we're doing Value Stream Mapping, we've had three different Lean Gurus teach us, we've sent people to college, we've created a Lean Team, and we've chosen a Lean Champion. We've tried everything we can think of and we're still not getting what we expect from Lean. We hear about companies who have made huge improvements but we can't seem to get it right! What are we missing? Why can't we make it stick?"*

This book is about answering that question. It's about discovering the missing piece of the sustainability puzzle. It's also about getting it right if it's your first time trying to implement Lean! If you're willing to listen, I have some ideas on how to either begin the process, or to make Lean stick after several tries. I've identified the critical elements and have developed a method that leads any organization through the process.

Recently, I did a search through all the Lean books on my shelf. Then I googled "Lean books". Every book that talked about "sustainability", or "sustaining Lean" mentioned "using the right tool" as the key. In fact, one of the most popular books talked about "Value Stream Mapping" as a critical component of Lean sustainability.

So I ask you, if Value Stream Mapping is so effective at sustainability, then why am I leading "Lean Culture" classes for companies who are highly effective at Value Stream Mapping? Because the tools are "not" the key to sustainability! Listening to people going on and on about the tools is kind of like hearing talk about the latest "get rich" scheme, or someone selling snake oil. Only in this case, the "snake oil" are tools that actually work. But they are definitely not the key to sustainability!

Everyone struggles with sustaining Lean, and it drives me crazy when I see people struggling. It means there are lost opportunities, lost jobs, frustrations, and wasted energy. It puts your organization in a difficult position. In today's economy, that could mean the beginning of the end.

You see, any organization is set up like a triangle, or pyramid. The top, or point, represents upper management – there are only a few of these people. The lower end of the triangle is wide – it represents the majority of people in the system. What we tend to do is focus on the top 20 percent and train them to within an inch of their life (top and middle management, supervisors, key support positions, etc.) We tell them that they are responsible for Lean and that they must drive it. It must start at the top, right? We create a Lean Champion or a Lean team and put them to work. We then give token attention or focus to the remaining 80 percent. Then, when Lean doesn't immediately take root, we force it. We start giving orders. It's at that point that people start rebelling. Or we get a great start, but when our work load increases, Lean goes out the window.

If we do our math, last time I checked, 80 percent trumps 20 percent. That's not even the new math. The 80 percent can clog up the works. It's frustrating, isn't it, when people don't "get it" when we think they should? Now, I can hear you say, *"Wait a minute, we run this company! We're the leaders! They have to do what we say! Why don't they do what they're told?"*

Therein lies the issue. You need to stop "telling people what to do!" You need everyone with you willingly, not just the 20 percent. Every person must make the decision to join in. That takes a different approach. An approach that you may not be used to. If you doubt me, I have a question for you: *What methods have you used to this point and how are they working for you?* If you don't like your results, you must change your methods!

This book is about helping you improve your methods to achieve ridiculously amazing results. It's about re-starting Lean one more time, the final time...and about making it stick.

My Definition of Lean

I think it's important to define the word Lean before we begin. This eliminates some confusion and possible frustration just in case our definitions don't match. Let's all get on the same page before we begin.

The reason I'm concerned with this is because there are many definitions for Lean floating around. Also, I know some of you hate the word Lean. So we'll look at some alternatives.

Some thoughts and definitions:
1. I use the word Lean because it is such a universally accepted word. Rather than play games, I just use it. You may call it whatever you want.
2. The word Lean could just as easily be called:
   - Continuous improvement
   - Productivity improvements
   - Common sense
   - Good business
3. The word Lean has some negative and some limiting connotations:
   - Some people think that Lean refers to only manufacturing, or the production floor, not to the office or service organizations. This likely started when we called it "Lean Manufacturing".

- Some people equate Lean to layoffs or getting rid of people.
- Some people equate Lean to foreign interference in our country.
- Some people think Lean is management's manipulation to get them to do more for little or no more pay, while management gets huge bonuses.

4. My definitions of Lean:
   - Manufacture (produce) only what the customer wants – only in the quantities they want – only when they want it – by only doing those things that add value.
   - Identify and eliminate waste in every area and in every process.
   - Produce only what is required by the downstream process, when it is required. No more, no less, no sooner.

5. In fact, Lean can be used by any person, in any job, in any organization.

Overview

of

The Six Laws of Lean

The Six Laws of Lean

Many times we get enamored with "how" we're doing something. We've done the homework and made our decision on how to proceed. Then, when it's not working the way we wanted it to work, we blame everything but our method.

Initially, we need to look at our present methods and ask how they're flawed. Many times change occurs because we've come to the conclusion that our present methods are not working. We're frustrated and maybe a little angry. Maybe our pride gets in the way because we can't stand to be wrong, especially if we were the one to create the present method. We don't like to admit we were wrong, do we? It's difficult to willingly accept the fact that what you're doing isn't working.

Is what you're doing working? Have you accepted the fact that it doesn't matter who's right or wrong? What matters are the results! The knowledge and acceptance that you're present methods are not working must fuel your drive to find the new method.

So in our approach to Lean, where do we go wrong? Why can't we get it to stick? Where's the flaw? What's the missing piece to the puzzle? To answer that question, I want to list what I think are the six laws of Lean, in order of importance:

- Law #1: Lean requires that you take everyone with you.
- Law #2: Lean is a culture.
- Law #3: Lean must encompass every area.
- Law #4: Lean is a way of thinking.
- Law #5: Lean focuses on results, not activities.
- Law #6: Lean is a set of tools, or methods, for finding and eliminating waste.

You'll find an overview of the six laws on each of the next few pages. In addition, each of the six laws are dealt with in detail as chapter headings as you journey through this book. Each of these chapters will provide additional answers in your search for the missing piece of your Lean Sustainability puzzle.

Law #1: Lean requires that you take everyone with you.

Most Lean journeys begin with a handful of people getting trained in the Lean tools. They are then expected to drive the process. This approach typical fails because the majority of people who don't "get it" will sabotage any progress. Lean can't be sustained this way, and if you can't sustain Lean, you'll have to start over. The more times you re-start, the greater the chance of failure. You need to get it right or you'll lose the focus and buy-in from people. This means you must have a defined process of moving everyone, not just the chosen few, from where they are today, to where they need to be. This component is the most critical to sustainability. Also, each person needs time to "process" what they're seeing and hearing. Most people who walk into my Lean class for the first time really don't want to be there. They are there because they were told to come, not because they want to. That's a start, but sustainability won't happen without desire. If you can't sustain what you're doing, the costs, frustrations, and wasted energy could overwhelm you. The only way to truly sustain Lean is to take everyone with you.

Critical question: How do people feel about Lean in your organization? Are they wrapping their arms around it, or are they rejecting it?

Law #2: Lean is a culture.

Is there negative energy within your organization? It's no surprise to me if you say yes. Every organization has it. As common as it is, it is extremely difficult, if not impossible, to sustain Lean if this negative behavior dominates daily life in your organization. It creates an unbelievable waste of energy and is a huge drain of resources. This negative culture is the single biggest contributing factor to what holds any organization back. It prevents you from reaching your highest potential. It kills your bottom line. You want to be more competitive? Do something about it! Actions that reduce negative behavior must dominate your Lean Implementation plan.

Critical question: Does negative behavior exist and perhaps dominate daily life in your organization?

Law #3: Lean must encompass every area.

Contrary to what you hear, Lean is not just for production. In many organizations, very few people outside of production take part in the Lean process. When we begin training, several key players are missing, which is obvious to everyone. Lean then falters right out of the gate. Or, support people come to the first class and then conveniently don't come back because they're "busy". Result? Lean fails. If you disagree, consider this: Some of the biggest problems (or opportunities for improvement) that I see in any organization occur in systems created by people in the office. On the other hand, I've seen wonderful processes fail because people in the affected area on the floor were never involved, because it's "not their job" to define the process. In reality, everyone must be involved. It's not optional.

Critical question: Is everyone, front to back, involved in Lean training and activities? Are they involved in the improvement of the processes they work within?

Law #4: Lean is a way of thinking.

One of the most difficult aspects of the Lean transition is taking your veterans with you. These are people who helped get you to where you are today and can be found in every department. And now you're asking them to change. That's tough for them to do. It doesn't make sense to them. That's why you must help them change the "way they think." And yes, there are ways to do that. If your veterans have not changed the "way they think", you've got trouble. Remember, the 80 percent trump the 20 percent. The roots of this law begin in Laws #1 and #2. Again, these people must "want to". Once they actively join in, they must learn to "see" waste, to always search for a better way, and to always ask the question, *"What's the best way to do this..."*

Critical question: Have your veterans changed the "way they think?"

Law #5: Lean focuses on results, not activities.

In trying to implement Lean, many people focus on activities (using the tools) rather than results. Remember the goal is not to use a tool, but to improve. No matter how you do it, Lean must help you create higher quality, improve on-time delivery, lower costs, improve safety...In other words, it better help you become more competitive... Right? Too often, people try to force the use of a tool and lose their focus. You must identify your objectives and create a scoreboard so everyone can see the results at all times.

I struggled with making this Law #5. It really should come first. Who plays a game without keeping score? The fact that I made it Law #5 tells you how important the first four laws are to your success. Also, the scoreboard comes a little later sequentially in your Lean Journey.

Critical questions: Has your approach, or "what" you do, become more important than the results?

Law #6: Lean is a set of tools, or methods, for finding and eliminating waste.

There are many tools that can be used to implement Lean. We tend to get enamored with some, to the exclusion of others. Witness that several years ago "Kaizen Events" dominated the scene. Now it's "Value Stream Mapping". That doesn't mean that these tools are bad, but the tool you use must fit the situation you're in. I see too many people using the wrong tools or force fitting a tool and becoming frustrated. They then say, *"Lean doesn't work!"* You must have a tool box full of tools, each of them designed to do different things. The best tool is usually the easiest to use and doesn't solve a problem that's not there. Also, you don't want the cure to be worse than the disease ever was.

Critical question: Are you using the correct tools? Does the tool fit the situation?

How We Get it Wrong

Have you discovered where we get it wrong? Look at the six laws again, in what I think are their order of importance:

- Law #1:   Lean requires that you take everyone with you.
- Law #2:   Lean is a culture.
- Law #3:   Lean must encompass every area.
- Law #4:   Lean is a way of thinking.
- Law #5:   Lean focuses on results, not activities.
- Law #6:   Lean is a set of tools, or methods, for finding and eliminating waste.

Notice the last one, the "tools of Lean?" I've put that last in importance. Where do most of us put it? That's right! We put it number one. The first thing we do is train people in the use of the tools and then we wonder why they don't "get it". That's because we put the cart before the horse.

Recently, I read an article that someone e-mailed me on "Decoding the DNA of the Toyota Production System". Separated from this title and the text, almost as a sub-title, was this phrase:

> *The Toyota story has been intensively researched and painstakingly documented, yet what really happens inside the company remains a mystery. Here's new insight into the unspoken rules that give Toyota its competitive edge."*

They then spend the entire article talking about four rules that are supposedly unwritten – all of them technical in nature.

What? Do you think that Toyota would hold something back? Do you think that Toyota is doing something that even they can't articulate? I don't think so! Everyone tries to copy Toyota and ends up frustrated! That's because two things are true: 1) You can't copy Toyota because you're not Toyota, and 2) The secret to Toyota is the people, not the technical stuff, even though the technical stuff is integral to the process.

Here is the main thought behind applying Lean and getting Lean to stick:

If people want to, they will.
If people don't want to, they won't.

I have found that if you start with the tools, people "won't". But if you lead them to a point where they "want to", they will. If people "want to" they'll get things done without even knowing the tools.

I have people tell me, even before they experience my approach, that all they need is for me to "teach their people the tools of Lean. We don't need any "touchy, feely" stuff. We don't need "teamwork" training." So I teach their people the Lean tools, and guess what? These people don't "want to". They don't "get it". I feel like I'm throwing stuff against the wall, hoping some of it sticks. I've developed some pretty good methods to teach the tools so that some of the "desire" to do it rubs off, but it's not the way to truly sustain it. And, I usually don't get everyone in front of me. So, the people who aren't there sabotage the outcome behind the scenes.

What I'm describing here is how we get it wrong. We put the cart before the horse. We skip critical steps in the process. We think we can score without touching all the bases. We simply teach the tools without laying any foundation. We assign a Lean team and after a year or two it fizzles out. Are you getting the results you want from your Lean efforts? Are you thinking you've got it wrong?

I suspect that you'll find out what most do when they experience the process I use. They come to me after the first session and they say, *"This is what we're missing!*

We've tried Lean so many times and we've never done it this way! It now makes perfect sense! We need your help!"

So, if you are frustrated with where you're at in your Lean journey, you've come to the right place. But, you better be open to a different approach. I've honed and refined this approach over 34 years in and around business. It works! If you follow my lead, it can change your life. If you think it's crazy, it'll take too much time, and it can't work, you'll probably be right.

The methods I use must be experienced. That can't happen by reading a book alone. However, this book examines the theory behind what I do. You see, it all has to do with people. The answer has been there all the time, but most don't see it, or they ignore it, or they think that Toyota somehow has a secret they're not sharing.

So, if what I'm saying makes some sense to you, let's continue the journey.

Law #1

Lean Requires that You take Everyone with You

Law #1: Lean Requires that You take Everyone with You

Lean sustainability means that you are able to sustain both the Lean process and Lean improvements into the future. Sustainability must be planned, implemented and measured if it has a chance to succeed. Lean sustainability begins and ends with taking everyone with you. Not just a certain few... all of them. Rather than worrying if people have the latest Value Stream Map completed, worry about if they "get it". Believe me, no company has gone out of business because a Value Stream Map wasn't done correctly. I venture to guess that most of the companies who go out of business, or fail to reach their potential, do so because many of their people "don't get it"!

Ok, so that's too melodramatic. Fine. Is everyone in your organization working to their full potential? Does everyone have a desire to make things better? Is that desire evident in everything they do? Do you feel like you're running a day care center? Does it seem like you're the only one who cares?

I was providing training in how to read blueprints to a group of hourly people at a local manufacturer recently. The subject turned to competition and the need for more detailed and accurate information. The group began to discuss all the internal problems with

Got Lean? Law #1

their blueprints, the communication within the plant, and all the people in the office that didn't have a clue.

So I said, *"Okay, I'll bite. What would you do about these things if you had a chance to change them?"*

They had all kinds of ideas, many of which made lots of sense to me! The main thought that I got from how they responded was that here was a group that cared! But they were frustrated!

I asked them if they had been involved in any Lean training and if they were expected to help solve these problems. They all laughed at me!

One guy said with feeling, *"Listen to us? You've got to be kidding! They're the experts and we're nothing but a bunch of pee-ons! We've got a Lean team that comes out here and tells us what to do. We're just expected to keep our mouths shut and do what we're told!"*

The sad part of this story is two fold. First of all, here was a great group of talented people who want to help, but are instead wasting their energy every day. Second, I had recently had a conversation with a senior executive in that organization who told me point blank that he didn't think my methods were what they needed. He felt that the Lean team and the engineers just weren't using the tools effectively.

Wow...there are none so blind as those that refuse to see! What an incredible waste of energy and talent!

See what I mean? Most organizations I begin working with are operating at less than 50 percent of their potential. The waste of time, energy, and space is hidden because of people who don't "get it". They really have no desire to change things. After all, they've been successful doing it the current way for years. This could include anyone, or any group, anywhere in the organization. But you know very well that competition shines a bright light on your performance. The goal of sustainability begins by the transformation of each person from the reality of today, or "not getting it", to where they need to be, or "getting it". Organizations with people who "get it" are able to sustain Lean. Organizations with people who "don't get it" cannot sustain Lean.

The question then becomes, *"How do we transform from "not getting it" to "getting it?"*

The Barrier

The biggest barrier to people "getting it" is the fact that you've been successful in the past using the methods you're using. So people ask, *"Why change?"* They see no need. In fact, your people may be holding you hostage! Your veterans control much of the information and processes you currently use. So you can do whatever you want...none of it will work until these veterans choose to make the changes necessary. In their minds you're crazy to want change... You don't know what you're talking about, especially if you've never done their job. I've also seen situations in which the change you're demanding is taken as a show of disrespect...a personal attack on them. In most organizations, your successful past may be the biggest barrier of people who don't "get it". Again, this hostage taking can be accomplished by any person or team, anywhere in the organization.

This is where most organizations fail in their Lean journey. They cannot sustain what they start because they keep slamming into this barrier of people who don't "get it". It forces them to start the process over and over again, only to see it fizzle. Your Lean journey is in jeopardy until you find a way to take everyone with you.

Your theoretically perfect goal for "Law #1" is:

> Take everyone along on your Lean journey.

Forget Lean "tools" for a moment and focus on people. Only people will get you where you need to go. Are your people spectators or participants?

Got Lean?   Law #1

Desire

Why do people do what they do? Because they want to! Notice what happens when a person doesn't want to do something. They drag their feet, they find every excuse not to do it (any excuse will do), they appear lazy, they procrastinate, and then when forced, they do it halfway. Leads you to think you should have just done it yourself!

Does this describe at least some of your people? So, let's introduce some Lean concepts and tools to this group. Sounds like fertile ground for Lean to grow doesn't it? Not!! And yet that's what many of us do...it's exactly where many Lean journeys begin.

So, if people do things because they want to, how do we get them to want to do Lean? Because if they want to...if they have a desire to...they will. Desire is the critical component. That's where we need to spend our valuable time. If people have a desire to do something, you better get out of their way. They will overcome every obstacle in their way. They'll do whatever it takes. They'll lie, cheat, steal...well, ok, you get the picture, right? There's no stopping a person bent on doing something. Desire is the rocket fuel that will propel your organization into the future.

Got Lean? Law #1

I remember a new group of people who were attending the first session of my Lean Culture class. They had never met me and I had never met them. After going through some brief introductory stuff, sign ins, and logistics, I began the session. Almost immediately, a technical person raised his hand and asked, with a smug look on his face, *"So, have you ever worked on the machines we use?"* Some of the people in the room had the good grace to look chagrined, but most of them looked like they wanted to cheer! The look on their faces, said *"Hah! You've got the guy trapped! Let's see him get out of this!"* I immediately raised one hand and gave them the "zero" sign, and said *"Zero"*. It's always fun doing this because it instantly deflates the group. As it did this one. I guess they thought I was going to make something up and then they could chase me around the parking lot a few times as I left running with my tail between my legs. Then I asked him, *"So, what's your point? Why would that make a difference?"*

He replied, *"Well, you're going to tell us what to do, but you don't have a clue about what we do, right?"*

The group loved that! They thought he had me on that one! Pictures of several more laps around the parking lot likely ran through their heads. So I asked him, *"Why would I tell you what to do? You're right, I don't know what you do and I wouldn't be so disrespectful as to presume that I do! That's not why I'm here!"*

I personally love that moment...when they're all confused...not knowing what I'm up to...it's a truly magical moment. Whether they realize it or not, it's the point at which they begin their own personal journey of change.

Creating Desire

Can you create desire in another person? It might be helpful to look at the following illustration to better understand the dynamics:

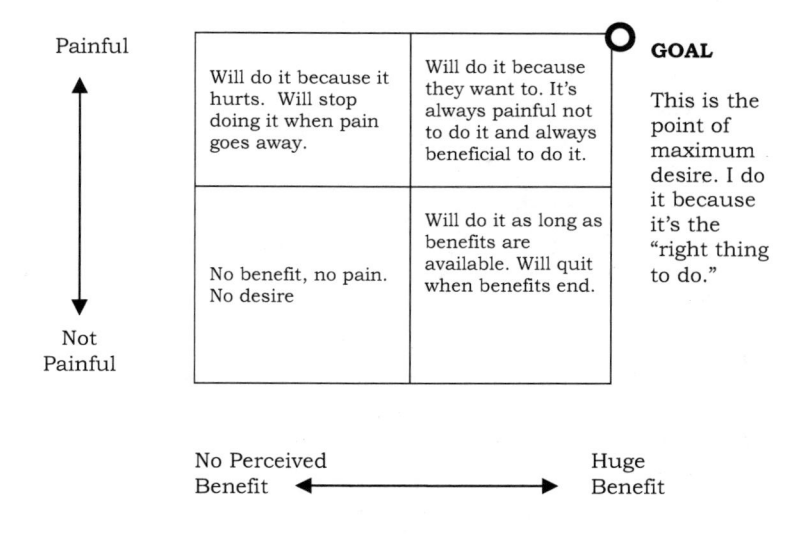

	Painful		
	Will do it because it hurts. Will stop doing it when pain goes away.	Will do it because they want to. It's always painful not to do it and always beneficial to do it.	**GOAL** — This is the point of maximum desire. I do it because it's the "right thing to do."
	No benefit, no pain. No desire	Will do it as long as benefits are available. Will quit when benefits end.	
Not Painful			

No Perceived Benefit ←——————→ Huge Benefit

Notice that in the lower left corner there is no pain and no benefit. This can create a person that has no desire.

Our goal is to assist people to reach the goal in the upper right hand corner, the point of "maximum desire". The more pain a person is in and the greater the perceived benefit, the greater the desire to change. In fact, when a person reaches the goal of "maximum desire", they reach a point where they do something because it's the right thing to do.

Notice the pain we introduce does not consist of threats and punitive measures. It is the honest sharing of information and challenging each person to be the best.

Introduce Pain. Share information:
- Threat of economy.
- Threat of competition.
- Consequences of not changing.
- Keep score.
- Set goals and objectives.
- Challenge people to step up.

Introduce Benefits.
- Ensuring future job.
- Beating the competition.
- Being the best.
- Healthy organization.

The question then becomes, *"What can we do to assist people in achieving 'maximum desire' to come along on the Lean journey?"* Here are some of the most important actions:

- **Give people a choice.** When people are not given a choice, they rebel. They fight what you're trying to do, even though it may end up making their life easier. It's a matter of control. If you take away a person's ability to control their situation they will search for whatever control they can grab hold of... usually negative. When people are given a choice and lots of good information, they will typically make the right choice on their own. And once they make that choice, things get a lot better because they're on board. Every person in your organization must answer the question, *"Is Lean a good thing, or is it a waste of time?"* Each person must answer this question for themselves. Not you...not their supervisor. With a solid Lean implementation process, you don't have to worry about the answer. People are smart. They'll make the right choice.

- **Follow a solid Lean implementation process.** It is difficult to put the process I use into words because it's something that has to be experienced. But your implementation must include all the elements found in this book, delivered in a hands-on, experiential, fun, challenging way. The person that leads this process must be credible and highly respected.

- **Give them time**. People need time to process and assimilate everything you're asking them to learn and do. You don't need to rush...you don't want to rush...it will sabotage your progress. If you have immediate issues within a certain area, deal with them separately. Don't drag the process down by throwing those issues into the middle and confusing everyone. There is no need to rush around like a chicken with your head cut off. Calm down. Follow the plan. Act like you're going to be in business for another 20 to 50 years. Don't act like you're at the OK Corral.

- **Help people understand how the business works**. I might be crazy, but how can people make good decisions and step up to implement changes when they don't know how the business operates? They need to understand things like competition, profit and loss, operating expenses, how much things cost...the list is seemingly endless. Fully 90 percent of the people in front of me (and I see thousands each year) don't understand how the business operates. Teach them. Their entire perspective changes when they get a little Business 101. It usually takes me one hour to totally change their perspective. It's worth it!

- **Share information with them.** Things like customer information, competitor threats, the economy, technology changes, cost overruns, process changes and anything else that helps them gain perspective and make good decisions.

- **Involve them.** I can give you many examples of how everyone but the hourly person is involved in the discussion of changes on a machine, or with a job. And when everyone else walks away, the hourly person, or team, must deal with how it's not working and all the problems associated with it. That same hourly person is many times the one with the critical idea that transforms or fixes what's wrong. Don't leave people out. It's disrespectful.

- **Don't blow smoke.** People are smart. They know when you're blowing smoke at them. Be honest, work with integrity, respect others, earn their trust, and share information. Surprisingly great things then have a chance to occur.

- **Flavor of the month.** People get frustrated when directions are changed on a frequent basis. It drives them crazy. It happens when someone at the top reads a book or goes to a seminar. Then, suddenly we shift to that new method. It's called "Flavor of the Month" or "Book of the Month Club". We must have consistency or results will suffer.

- **Respect people**. All of the things mentioned so far will show respect. More on respect later. Note: Respect is the most ridiculously important concept in this entire book.

- **Some may not be happy**. Taking everyone with you doesn't mean that you try to keep everyone happy... That will never work. I make lots of decisions that don't necessarily make me happy, but it's the right thing to do. So do you. You want people to do the right thing. It's not just about "keeping them happy".

Ownership

Most organizations run on the theory of compliance. We tell people what to do and they do it. The big problem with this is that you get performance to a minimum standard. That will never make you the "best". Taking everyone with you involves people willingly going along. People who "get it" don't just comply. They "own" what's happening. Ownership is the theory that must replace compliance. Desire creates ownership, the only path to becoming the "best". With ownership comes energy and focus.

Every person in your organization must "own" the objective. Some thoughts on this:
- People who own the objective, "get it"!
- People who own the objective make good decisions.
- People who own the objective get things done.
- People who own the objective overcome obstacles that get in their way.
- People who own the objective have a burning desire to be the best.

It would seem, then, that we ought to identify this objective. Here are some ideas:

Overall objective: To be the best in the world at what we do.

Specific objective: To produce quality product or service, on time, at the least possible cost, in a safe manner, and have fun doing it.

The challenge for each person is to be the "best in the world" at their job. You must also challenge each person to a higher purpose than just "doing my job."

I'm sure you've heard the story of three people working on a project. When asked what they were working on, the first person said, *"I'm just doing what I'm told. I'm just doing my job"*. The second person said, *"I'm building this wall."* The third person said, *"I'm building a cathedral"* and went on to explain in great detail how many people's lives would be changed because of it. This third person is a person that is passionate! Here's a person that "gets it".

90 percent of the people who sit in my class can't really articulate their objective. People in formal leadership positions can't always fully articulate it either. That's not good! Here are the four levels of ownership of the objective:

Level One: Don't know it. Don't own it. Don't care. Just give me my paycheck.

Level Two: These are the book smart people. They can easily spit out the objective. They know the words, especially in front of the boss. But, when you watch them work you can tell they don't own it. Not even close.

Level Three: Here are people who want to own the objective and they do a pretty good job of it. They just can't articulate it very well.

Level Four: This group owns the objective. They discuss how to improve what they're doing to reach it. They continually work toward perfection and excellence in everything they do.

Your goal is to challenge everyone to reach level four. Spend the bulk of your time helping people "own" the objective. Once this happens they will also own the improvement process! It will create a passion for what they're doing! Everything in this book will assist in putting people in a position of owning the objective! Bottom line: If people own the objective, own the improvement process, and are passionate about what they're doing, it's a safe bet that you've "taken them with you"!

Conclusion

The information in this section about "taking everyone with you" forms one of the foundational elements in sustaining your Lean progress and moving forward to ever increasing levels of excellence. Think of it as the foundation at the base of the wall. It must be solid to hold everything up. I would even say that Lean is, at best, crippled without this foundation, and at worst, it may not stick at all. It should be your first discussion prior to attempting to implement Lean in your

Got Lean? Law #1

organization. Choose to ignore it, gloss over it, or rush through it at your own peril.

Critical concepts learned in this chapter:
1. Take everyone with you on the Lean journey.
2. Grow people that "get it".
3. Assist people to reach a goal of "maximum desire", or people who "want to".
4. Give people a choice.
5. Follow a solid Lean implementation process.
6. Give people time to process and assimilate.
7. Help people understand how the business operates.
8. Share information freely.
9. Involve people in the improvement of the processes that affect them.
10. Don't blow smoke at people.
11. Be consistent in your approach. Don't do "Flavor of the Month" or "Book of the Month Club".
12. Respect people.
13. Remember, you may not be able to make everyone happy.
14. Help people "own" the objective.
15. Compliance must be replaced by ownership.

Got Lean? Law #1

Practice Exercise: Law #1

Complete the following and check your answers with the answer sheet found on page 57. Do not treat this as a test. The goal is not to get a high grade, but to get them all correct. If you don't know an answer, look back through the materials to find it.

1. A critical question asked by Law #1 is:
    a. Do our people do what they're told?
    b. Do our people "get it"?
    c. Can we hide our true motive of getting people to do more for less money?
    d. How fast can we get improvements through Lean implementation?
    e. A and C

2. Simply "telling people what to do" will achieve:
    a. Ownership of the objective.
    b. Desire within each person to get things done.
    c. A great method of overcoming obstacles.
    d. Compliance to a minimum standard.
    e. B and C.

3. Most people cannot articulate the _____.

4. People who "get it" _____ the objective.

5. Lean sustainability begins and ends with:
    a. Ownership of the objective.
    b. Using Lean tools effectively.
    c. Taking everyone with you.
    d. Effective implementation of Value Stream Mapping.
    e. B and D.

6. The point of "maximum desire" is the goal of:
    a. Someone doing something because it's the right thing to do.
    b. Introducing maximum pain to achieve desire.
    c. Introducing a huge benefit to achieve desire.
    d. The supervisor or manager shaking up the troops to get more done.
    e. B and C.

7. People rebel when you take away their:
    a. Donuts.
    b. Flavor of the month.
    c. Objective.
    d. Freedom of choice.
    e. None of the above.

8. Ownership of the objective creates:
    a. Smart alecks.
    b. Energy.
    c. Compliance.
    d. Focus.
    e. B and D.

9. Challenging people to a higher purpose than just "doing my job" creates:
     a. A passionate person who gets it.
     b. A person who sees the bigger picture.
     c. A person who owns the objective.
     d. Lean sustainability.
     e. All of the above.

10. Lean implementation takes time because:
     a. Lean tools can't be implemented quickly.
     b. It's difficult to know where to start.
     c. People need time to process and assimilate.
     d. There are so many obstacles.
     e. A and B.

11. Successful Lean implementation depends on keeping every person happy.
     a. True.
     b. False.

12. People who own the objective:
     a. Get things done.
     b. Make good decisions.
     c. Wait around for someone to tell them what to do.
     d. Overcome obstacles that get in their way.
     e. A, B, and D.

Law #1: Lean Requires that You take Everyone with You

Self Assessment

No				Yes		
1	2	3	4	5	1)	Have we taken everyone with us?
1	2	3	4	5	2)	Do our people "get it"?
1	2	3	4	5	3)	Are we assisting in creating desire?
1	2	3	4	5	4)	Do we give people a choice?
1	2	3	4	5	5)	Are we following a solid Lean implementation process?
1	2	3	4	5	6)	Do we give people time to process and assimilate?
1	2	3	4	5	7)	Do we assist people in understanding how the business operates?
1	2	3	4	5	8)	Do we share information freely?
1	2	3	4	5	9)	Do we involve people in the improvement process?
1	2	3	4	5	10)	Do we blow smoke at people?
1	2	3	4	5	11)	Are we consistent in our approach?
1	2	3	4	5	12)	Do we respect people?
1	2	3	4	5	13)	Have we gotten beyond just trying to make everyone happy?
1	2	3	4	5	14)	Do we help people "own" the objective?
1	2	3	4	5	15)	Have we replaced compliance with ownership?

Law #1: Lean Requires that You take Everyone with You

Group Discussion Questions

1. Given the self assessment questions on the previous page, what are your organization's:

    Strengths:

    Weaknesses:

2. What can you do to help people "own" the objective?

3. Why is it critical that every person understands how the business operates?

4. What is the percentage of people in your organization that "get it" versus "don't get it?"
    Get it? _____%   Don't get it _____%
    What impact does this have on your competitiveness?

5. Discuss the importance of "taking everyone with you".

Got Lean? Law #1

Practice Exercise Answer Sheet

1. B
2. D
3. Objective
4. Own
5. C
6. A
7. D
8. E
9. E
10. C
11. B
12. E

Law #2

Lean Is a Culture

Law #2: Lean Is a Culture

One organization I began working with included everyone in the training process, except for the owner. Why? He didn't think what we were doing made any sense. In his words, *"why should another consultant be able to help, when the first five failed?"* The Plant Manager put his job on the line to bring me in. (I didn't know I was the 5th at the time). We divided everyone into eight groups. The first group was the 3rd shifters who were already in the room when I walked in for our 5:00 a.m. class. One of the guys said to me as I walked in, *"You don't need to put down your stuff! You won't be here long! We don't want any part of what you're gonna say!"* I guess they thought I'd turn tail and run out of the building screaming or something! I proceeded to make a big show of putting down my stuff. (Have you noticed yet that I love a challenge?) Then I looked at them, motioned them toward me, and said, *"Bring it on!"* I'll tell you, it was one of the biggest challenges of my life. It was as if someone took me to a rodeo, strapped me on a steer and opened the gate. We met every week for 18 months and talked pretty much exclusively of earning trust and respect...about challenging the positive people to take back the company. It took them the better part of two years to transform themselves. But they did it! About two years in I met the owner for the first time. He walked up to me, introduced himself, and said, *"I owe you an apology. Our attitudes and our bottom line have completely reversed. I didn't think your method had any chance of working, but I see now that it's the only method that truly works."* Here was an organization that was not even close to being able to use the tools when we began the process. They needed a new heart first!

Do you have a little negative energy within your organization? Bet you do! So how do you take everyone with you if your culture doesn't support it? How do you implement Lean if your culture doesn't support it? That's what Law #2 is all about. You must create a culture that is positive and encouraging, that nurtures and sustains Lean. The negative culture must be thrown out.

If "taking everyone with you" is the foundation (Law #1) then "Law #2: Lean is a Culture" is the mortar, or glue, that holds everything together. In fact, sustainability and culture are inseparable. They go hand-in-hand.

Your theoretically perfect goal for "Law#2" is:

> Create a positive culture in which it is possible for everyone to want to take responsibility for results.

Notice the wording in this goal? Just because you create a positive environment doesn't mean people will embrace it. Even in a perfect environment there are people who won't, or don't, take responsibility for results. But you must make every attempt! To accomplish this culture change each person must be challenged to look at their own behavior and skills. Many people have fallen into a trap of negative behavior, such as: whining, complaining, finger pointing, and general disrespect for both their peers and management. There are also occasions in which the negative energy is created and perpetuated by one or more people who hold a formal leadership position. As a result of either, or both of these, the rest of the people see no way out of this negative cycle and are so frustrated by it, they've become pessimistic, negative, cynical, and disrespectful. Your job is to provide the hope, the skills, the methods and the support required to break this negative, energy draining cycle.

Culture Change

What is the "culture" like in your organization? Is there a lot of complaining? I've found that there are varying degrees of a negative culture in every organization I walk into. The people who want to do something about it are frustrated because they can't seem to change it. Nothing seems to work. Most of these people have resigned themselves to thinking that nothing can be done. I meet a lot of frustrated, demoralized people who are sick of it, who can't see any light at the end of tunnel. But there is hope. Hope blooms when you begin to understand why this negative culture exists and what feeds it.

Culture change occurs when each person begins to understand, accept, and practice the following:

1. **Behavior is a choice.** You change your behavior first and attitude follows. It is difficult, if not impossible, to change your attitude quickly, but a behavior is fairly easy to change. Many people don't consciously choose their behavior...they just follow the crowd. If you are a negative person and you work in a negative environment, life becomes very difficult for you when you make a conscious decision to improve your behavior. You'll find yourself swimming upstream...against the current. So while behavior is easy to change in a positive environment, it is terrifically difficult to change in a negative environment. Everything and everybody seems to conspire to drag you down into the negative pit. That's why many negative people fail when making a conscious decision to behave positively. They can't overcome the negative undertow. Breaking this negative pull takes persistence and tenacity. That's why you begin by changing a few basic behaviors first. Choose your behavior and don't let anything or

anyone get in your way. Your attitude will follow along.

2. **Control what you can, not what you can't.** We must concentrate and work on what is in our control, not what is outside our control. We can only control ourselves – for most people this is a full time job, which means there should be no time to point fingers at others.

Yet, most people spend their time trying to control other people – and they find it difficult, frustrating, and virtually impossible. So if all of us are trying to control other people and not ourselves, what's actually happening? Nothing! If you spend your time trying to control others, then nothing is being done to control yourself. So in effect, "everyone" is standing around waiting for "everyone else" to change...and "nothing" is really happening! Nothing will happen until you look yourself in the mirror and take action on what you see needs to be changed within yourself. If you're like me, this is a full time job. You won't have time to worry about other people.

3. **Either influence or let it go.** If something is outside of our control we can either "influence", or we can "let it go". Influence occurs as we build relationships and earn the trust and

respect of other people. Interesting note – we are influenced by people we trust and respect, not by someone yelling, screaming, or whining in our ear. So if you want to "influence" someone, you must first build the relationship by earning their trust and respect – this takes time...you gotta "want to" really bad! So, if you want to influence someone to change their behavior, you must look yourself in the mirror... you must first change your behavior toward that person. You earn the opportunity to influence someone! But, underneath it all you must be ready and willing to let it go or it will eat you alive!

4. **Choose to respect others.** Each person must choose to respect other people even when it is difficult or when it appears to be undeserved. "You respect someone the most when they deserve it the least." Many organizations show little respect for the "lower" 80 percent of the organization. How? They don't include them in what's going on! They just tell them what to do, with no explanation. Many times, they are rude to them and treat them like second class citizens. This is a respect issue. Everyone must be treated like an owner!

5. **Trust is earned**. Don't worry if "other" people can be trusted. Worry about whether "you" can be trusted. Is trust important within your

organization? Absolutely! Do you have trust issues within your organization? More than likely! The question is, *"how do we grow trust?"* The answer: each person must "earn" the trust of other people through their behavior and the choices they make. Don't worry about someone else! If everyone does this even reasonably well, you can improve the level of trust dramatically.

6. **Nothing happens unless we "choose" to make it happen**. Desire begins the process. If you have no desire to change, you won't. No one can demand or force you – if they do, all they'll get is compliance to a minimum standard. I detest compliance! Compliance is not going to help us compete effectively. It won't help us become the "best" at what we do. With desire comes commitment and ownership- the only way to create excellence.

7. **Remember the "20-50-30" rule**. In a typical situation, 20 percent of the people are positive and willingly embrace changes. You can depend on them to help drive improvement. Another 50 percent are fence sitters. They're not hostile but they're not helping like they should either. The remaining 30 percent are negative. They resist any change and often deliberately try to make it fail. The 30 percenters are often the most vocal. They love to complain and love it when you give

them lots of attention. Their goal is to suck you into their negative pit.

Your goal is to recognize the 20 percent and feed them, identify the 50 percent and win them over, and don't let the 30 percent control you. If you feed the 20 percent and convert the 50 percent, you're 70 percent of the way. Many of the remaining 30 percent will convert when they see what's happening and when they start losing their power.

Note: When a 30 percenter starts to lose their power they will fight it. They'll get worse! I've had people tell me several weeks into the training that the negativity is worse than before! I just smile and tell them they have just seen evidence that they're moving in the right direction because the 30 percenters are feeling the pinch. Stay on course and don't let up!

I've seen the 30 percenters who lead the negative group lose their power in as little as four weeks. But that's unusual – it generally takes much longer than that. I've also had a union president tell me that her role was to be the "bitch". The union people expected her to fight for them. I spent hours trying to help her understand that she would accomplish a thousand times more using positive behavior than negative. Her heart told her that was true but her head never gave in. She never made the transition.

8. **Who runs your company?** Given the 20-50-30 rule, guess who runs your company? That's right – the 30 percenters! They dictate what happens and what doesn't happen. Doesn't that drive you crazy? It should!

How does that happen? We allow it! Here's how:

- The 20 percenters go about their business. They say, *"I don't control the behavior of other people. That's management's job."* And because we don't fully realize the impact, we let them off the hook.

- The 30 percenters are highly active and love an audience. Their most captive audience is the 50 percenters who are allowed to drift...remember, the 20 percenters are not pulling them in a positive direction. So the 50 percenters get pulled into the negative pit.

- Now we have a 80/20 split with the majority in the negative camp.

- The 20 percenters get so frustrated by the lack of progress and the inability to get things done that they either quit or join the negative camp in frustration.

The end result is a negative organization!

So how do you change this? First, if you are in a "formal" leadership position your job is to "feed the 20 percenters!" Spend most of your time with the 20 percenters...feed them...challenge them to step up to lead the organization. Also, challenge them to take the 50 percenters with them. Second, the 20 percenters must step up to lead in a positive direction. They must not be allowed to stick their heads in the sand.

9. **Choose to behave "positively"**. If you think that the transition to a positive culture isn't necessary, you need to ask yourself the following questions:

Question #1: "What has been your typical response to change, adversity, or something that concerns you...but that you can't control?"

Chances are it's been a negative, finger pointing, complaining, blaming response, right?

Note: In most organizations the only way to describe this behavior is with the words "bitching and complaining." I'm sorry for my language here, but I need to call it what it is! Most of us bitch and complain in this situation. Is this true of you? Is it true in your organization?

Question #2: "How long have you responded in this negative way?"

Most people tell me they've responded negatively "all their lives!"

Question #3: "So where's it gotten you?"

For most people, the answer is *"nowhere"* or *"here I am! My negative behavior has gotten me nowhere. In fact, I'm frustrated and angry!"*

Question #4: "So why do you continue to do something that doesn't work?"

Most people don't know how to respond to this at first. Some of the reasons include: we have formed habits, it's human nature to complain and blame others, we need to just "vent" sometimes, or maybe it works just often enough to seem viable.

Question #5: "Are you crazy?"

Do you know the definition of insanity? It is to "keep doing the same thing but expect different results".

So you're crazy if you think "more of the same" is going to change things. If this bitching and complaining has gotten you nowhere and you've used it all your life, you've got to try something different! If you still don't agree, think about this: "If you always do what you always did, you will always get what you always got." If you don't like what you've got, you need to do something different! You must choose to turn your negative behavior into positive behavior!

Beyond just habit, many people are negative simply because they don't see any other choice. But remember, you do have a choice. Choose to behave in a "positive" way.

10. **Positive behavior includes four basic decisions.** Choosing positive behavior involves making decisions. The decisions that make up positive behavior include:

   1. I will have fun.

   2. I will challenge myself... it's the best way to have fun!

   3. I will earn trust.

4. I will respect others.

Notice the "I will" part of each of these. When you say "I will", there is no wiggle room..."I will" means just that...it doesn't mean, *"well, I'll do it if everything goes well!"* When you say "I will" it means you've made a decision to do it.

If you're like me, this decision to behave positively is a full time job. "I will" also means that you keep the mirror on yourself, rather than finger point. If you can make these changes even "reasonably" well, your life will get better. If everyone...every person in your organization...chooses these behaviors...and does them "reasonably" well...you can together transform your organization! Many times the best response to someone who continues to bitch and complain, over and over, is to ask them point blank, *"How's that working for you?"*

I had a person stop me three months after he attended the class in which I covered the "four positive behaviors". He said he had left the class totally pumped up! He had this coworker who he just couldn't stand, so he decided to use the four positives, starting with earning trust and respecting this guy. I asked him how it was going.

His response? *"The guy treats me worse now then he did before!"* (He wasn't real happy when I started laughing). He asked me, *"What do I do?"*

"Look", I said, *"What difference does it make if he treats you worse?"*

"Well, because if he keeps it up, I'll just start treating him like he treats me!"

I looked him right in the eye and asked, *"So, where do think that will get you?"* He melted right in front of me! He knew that wouldn't accomplish anything besides making it worse, if that was possible. I had to explain to him again that he couldn't control someone else. He had made a decision on how he was going to treat this guy. He needed to stick with that decision because it was the right thing to do and not to worry so much about how this guy was responding. His response, *"Do you know how tough that is?"* Oh yes, I think I do! In fact, it may be the toughest thing any of us do!

11. **People who are constantly complaining don't have enough to do.** Whenever I see someone complaining, it's clear that they don't have enough to do. Check that. Actually, busy people still bitch and complain. The only way to convert a 50 or 30 percenter is to "challenge" them, or

put them in a situation that challenges them to use their skills in a positive way.

It was the first day in my new role as a supervisor many years ago. One of our senior technical people, Joe, who I had worked with for several years, came into my office and said, *"I'm going to be in here every month asking for more money. Money is the only thing that motivates me, so I'm going to bug you about it all the time."*

I looked at him and said, *"You're at the top of the pay scale! You're not getting a raise! Get back to work!"* True to his word, he came every month to bug me for a raise. It became a game, where I'd close my blinds and lock the door if I saw him coming.

One day I was trying to figure out who to put on a job that required a precise attention to detail. This job had huge potential and the person currently working on it just didn't have the right skill set.

In walks Joe. He sits in the chair next to my desk, and says, *"I'm here for my raise."* I said, *"Yea, yea, whatever. Who can we put on this job?"* I described what was needed to him, and as I talked, it dawned on me who should do that job! Him! So I told him, *"You're the guy! You can do this! I need you to do this!"* He balked and said, *"No way!"* I kept talking to him and told him to think about it. He came into my office three days later, and said, *"I'll do it!"*

Guess who never came into my office again asking for more money? When I "called" him on it a year later, he told me he was having too much fun to worry about it anymore! His words, not mine! Challenge a 30 percenter and watch the petty stuff begin to disappear!

12. **Change is the only constant.** So why do we need all this touchy-feely stuff? Because we must make changes to successfully compete in today's economy. Our competitors are not standing still. They put more pressure on us every day. So we must "force" change. So how do you "force" change with a group that doesn't want change?...in fact, they fight it every day! All I know is that you better have earned their trust and respect...and then you challenge them! An appropriate challenge "forces" positive change!

13. **Positive energy equals results.** How much energy is lost in your organization every week as a result of all the whining and complaining? How much more could you get done if this negative energy was turned into positive action? When I ask this question, most groups admit

that they could improve output by 20 to 80 percent!! Many organizations are frustrated because they can't compete. They have seemingly tried everything. Eventually, in frustration, they outsource – many times off shore. Given this situation, what if you could tap into this 20 – 80 percent waste created by negative energy? Could we then compete? Still think this touchy-feely stuff isn't important?

14. **Ground rules.** If you have a group that has a difficult time moving forward, can't agree, and lack respect, the following ground rules must be followed:

- It doesn't matter who's right and who's wrong.

- If you can't prove it, you can't state it as fact.

- Actively listen to other people. Asking questions is the best way to listen.

- Everyone has the right to disagree, but not to be disagreeable. Asking questions is the best way to disagree.

- Using a rational, structured process is the key to reaching our objective. Using the appropriate tool keeps you on track.

- Remember that knowledge and experience can work against you. It can create tunnel vision.

- If you don't have the facts, go get them. Don't discuss or argue. Get the facts, then discuss.

- Don't discuss or argue about an idea too long before simply trying it out.

15. **Hang out with other positive people.** In your quest to become a positive person, it is critically important who you hang out with. It's pretty difficult to be positive if you hang with negative people. Find other positive people, or 20 percenters, to hang with so that they can encourage and support you, and you them. Don't spend your valuable time listening to 30 percenters.

16. **Use excess energy wisely.** Everyone has excess energy. Are you using yours productively and positively? Or are you complaining, goofing off, trash talking, or wasting it? Tap into this excess energy to create positive change.

Conclusion

This chapter is on culture and how to create a positive culture within your organization. How can you expect people to step up to get things done when they are constantly being pulled into a negative pit? A positive culture is the glue that holds everything together. Without a positive culture, your ability to sustain a Lean organization is greatly diminished.

Critical concepts learned in this chapter:

1. Create a positive culture in which it is possible for everyone to want to take responsibility for results.

2. Build relationships by earning the trust and respect of every person you work with.

3. Choose your behavior and don't let anything or anyone get in your way.

4. Choose to respect every person – treat everyone like you do the owner or a valued customer.

5. Influence if you can, let it go if you can't.

6. Trust is earned, not given.

7. Challenge yourself and others to higher levels of excellence.

8. Feed the 20 percenters and challenge them to lead.

9. Take the 50 percenters and 30 percenters with you.

10. Recognize that negative behavior doesn't work.

11. Choose to behave positively. Choose to have fun, challenge yourself, earn trust, and respect others.

12. People who constantly complain have not been challenged effectively.

13. Change is the only constant. Deal with it!

14. Positive energy equals results.

15. Follow the ground rules.

16. Hang out with other positive people.

17. Use excess energy wisely.

If every person chooses these behaviors and practices them continually, you can change your organization in a profound and lasting way.

Practice Exercise: Law #2

Complete the following and check your answers with the answer sheet found on page 86. Do not treat this as a test. The goal is not to get a high grade, but to get them all correct. If you don't know an answer, look back through the materials to find it.

1. Law #2 talks of a culture that is:
    a. The glue that holds everything together.
    b. Rewarding to people in support positions.
    c. Positive and encouraging.
    d. Conducive to the Lean team.
    e. A and C.

2. If you want to improve trust, each person must:
    a. Insist on it.
    b. Earn it.
    c. Point out the faults of others.
    d. Expect management to dictate it.
    e. C and D.

3. Who basically "runs" your company?
    a. 20 percenters.
    b. 50 percenters.
    c. 30 percenters.
    d. The HR Department.
    e. The customer.

Got Lean?   Law #2

4. Your behavior must be a _____.

5. You _____ the opportunity to influence someone.

6. Many groups will admit that output will increase by 50 percent if:
    a. The negative energy is changed to positive energy.
    b. We create a Lean team.
    c. They are given a big pay increase and more vacation time.
    d. The 30 percenters are fired after being flogged.
    e. Their supervisor is sent to a country involved in a civil war.

7. The best way to actively listen to other people is to:
    a. Shut your mouth.
    b. Act interested.
    c. Take notes.
    d. Ask questions.
    e. Nod your head a lot.

8. If you create a positive culture, every person will embrace it.
    a. True.
    b. False.

Got Lean? Law #2

9. Positive behavior involves:
    a. Concessions.
    b. Priorities.
    c. Decisions.
    d. Getting rid of some people.
    e. A and B.

10. The only way to shut up a 30 percenter is to:
    a. Challenge them.
    b. Write them up.
    c. Keep them busy.
    d. Torture them.
    e. Tell them you heard that they were getting fired.

11. Most people spend their time:
    a. Trying to make other people look bad.
    b. Trying to look busy.
    c. Complaining about management.
    d. Trying to control other people.
    e. Trying to look good to their supervisor.

12. 20 percenters must:
    a. Step up to create a positive culture.
    b. Take the 50 percenters with them.
    c. Lead in a positive way.
    d. Assist in taking back control of the organization from the 30 percenters.
    e. All of the above.

Got Lean?   Law #2

13. You respect someone the most when they _____ it the least.

14. The best way to have fun is to _____ yourself.

15. If your complaining hasn't got you what you want, you must:
    a. Do more complaining. That should help.
    b. Try something else.
    c. Blame someone else.
    d. Commit yourself. You're going crazy.
    e. A and D – they go hand in hand.

Law #2: Lean is a Culture

Self Assessment

No				Yes		
1	2	3	4	5	1)	Have we created a positive culture in which it is possible for everyone to want to take responsibility for results?
1	2	3	4	5	2)	Are we building relationships by earning trust and respect?
1	2	3	4	5	3)	Do we truly respect each person?
1	2	3	4	5	4)	Are you earning trust?
1	2	3	4	5	5)	Are you challenging people to higher levels of positive behavior?
1	2	3	4	5	6)	Are you feeding the 20 percenters?
1	2	3	4	5	7)	Are the 20 percenters taking the 50 and the 30 percenters with them? Are they actively leading?
1	2	3	4	5	8)	Have we recognized that negative behavior is killing our bottom line?
1	2	3	4	5	9)	Are people choosing to behave positively?
1	2	3	4	5	10)	Have you challenged people who complain?
1	2	3	4	5	11)	Are you following the ground rules?
1	2	3	4	5	12)	Are you hanging with positive people?

Law #2: Lean is a Culture

Group Discussion Questions

1. Given the self assessment questions on the previous page, what are your organization's:

    Strengths:

    Weaknesses:

2. What can we do to help people "choose" positive behavior?

3. Why is it critical for every person to build positive relationships?

4. What is the percentage of people in your organization that fill each of the 20-50-30 categories? Discuss the differences in how each of you responded, and the impact of your findings on your organization.
    20% _____% 50% _____% 30% _____%

5. Discuss the importance of creating a culture in which it is possible for everyone to want to take responsibility for results.

Got Lean?   Law #2

Practice Exercise Answer Sheet

1. E
2. B
3. C
4. Choice
5. Earn
6. A
7. D
8. B
9. C
10. A
11. D
12. E
13. Deserve
14. Fun
15. B

Law #3

Lean Must Encompass Every Area

Law #3: Lean Must Encompass Every Area

I thought long and hard before adding this as a Law. We've talked at length about the need to take everyone with you. It stands to reason, then, that Lean would encompass every area, because people fill positions and job titles. If every position is filled, and everyone goes along, then Lean would encompass every area.

I added it, though, because this is another point at which I think organizations get it wrong. So forgive me if it seems redundant, or doesn't seem important enough. I think it's terrifically important and needs to be highlighted.

Mistake #1

Many Lean journeys begin with the Management Team picking a person or team to drive the process. This Lean Champion or Lean Team is charged with implementing Lean throughout the organization. They receive Lean training and get to work. Within a year or two the Lean journey falters because they cannot sustain any progress. The bulk of the organization is looking at them with their thumbs in their ears, waggling their fingers, and saying, *"How's that working for you?"*

As we've seen in the first two Laws of Lean, this approach spells trouble. Again, it's difficult to sustain Lean if you don't take everyone with you.

Mistake #2

In this chapter, we'll look at another mistake many organizations make when implementing Lean. If and when they discover that more people need to be involved in the process, they make a fatal mistake: they allow some people to opt out. Typically the production people, floor associates, or hourly people are involved in this next attempt at Lean, but office and support people are allowed to skip. Several reasons for this include that these people:

- Are not viewed as integral to the process.
- Are not viewed as the problem, while hourly people are.
- Are viewed as professional, and should not be lumped in with hourly people.
- Feel they are a step above an hourly person.
- Feel that Lean is production focused and they are not in the production area.

In a Lean class, not long ago, I had a bookkeeper who asked me why she was included in the Lean training. I had just given them the textbook definition of Lean and she equated the definition to a production environment. Her point? *"Why do I need to be here if it doesn't involve me?"*

I asked her, *"Why do you think it doesn't involve you?"* She responded, *"Because I don't run production!"* I asked her, *"How does this organization make its money?"* Since it was a manufacturing company, the obvious answer was that they make their money selling quality product at the least possible cost.

So I said to her and the group, *"Since this is a manufacturing company, every person has the same overall goal... to produce quality product at the lowest possible cost... we don't make money doing the books, do we?* (I hope not!) *If you want to make money doing the books you need to go work for an accounting firm. That's what they do for a living. Here, we produce quality product at the lowest possible cost."*

The issue, of course, is that she didn't "get it". She didn't want any part of Lean. The good news is that she did end up getting it. She made the transformation and implemented many improvements that reduced or eliminated waste in the accounting department.

In another class, I had a receptionist raise her hand and say *"I love what we're doing here, and I would love to stay, but I don't know how this pertains to me!"*

Here was a person who wanted to get it. It didn't take long for her to find out that she was gifted and skilled at organizing things. She took on the office supplies room, even though it wasn't her responsibility. She did it because she wasted lots of time every week looking for things when people would stop by her desk and ask, *"Do we have any permanent markers? I can't seem to find any!"*

When she started organizing this office supplies room, things fell off the shelf when you opened the door. It was a mess! By the time she got done, the room and everything in it was so organized and easy to find, it brought tears to your eyes. This room was sustained for several years, and still is, because the process, or how it was organized, was so good, and the fact that she is extremely respected by everyone. Nobody wanted to mess it up!!

So, I ask you, who else could have made this improvement but her?" This was one of her things to do! No one else would have done it, or could have done it better! Here's a person who gets it! But in most organizations this won't happen unless someone else does it, or perhaps she wouldn't have been permitted to do it in the first place!

The theoretically perfect goal for "Law #3" is:

> Every position and job title must be actively involved
> in the Lean process.

My evidence to support this law? Many of the worst, most wasteful, processes I find in any organization were created by someone in the office.

Generally speaking, people in office and support positions "create" processes, and people in hourly positions "implement" those processes. Each position must be appropriately involved in a process and its improvement: if the creators don't follow and implement Lean practices, the created process could be full of waste. If the implementers don't use Lean practices, the process may never be improved. In fact, I can give you many examples of where people who design processes, and those who must implement them, don't even talk to each other. How much waste could we find in that situation? How much you want to bet that their processes could be improved? Too many times people struggle to be competitive using a flawed process. And when they say something about it, they are told they have an attitude problem. Or told, "*What do you know about anything*". Remember also that this can work both ways. At the root of this issue is a lack of respect, being territorial, or a cover up for weak or missing skills.

Blur the Lines

The best organizations have the ability to get everyone appropriately involved. Every person involved in a project and its implementation must focus their energy on creating and improving that process. Everyone should be transparent. There are no positions, just responsibilities. It doesn't matter who's right and wrong. Facts are always pursued, rather than letting emotions control actions. There are no hidden agendas. Every person is respected and valued, no matter their job title, how educated they are, or what clothes they wear.

Remember that the success of your organization is vitally important to everyone, not just certain people. If people have an attitude problem, help them change it. If someone is not skilled at something, help them learn the skill.

Perfect Attendance

To take everyone along and also to encompass people from every area of the organization, perfect attendance at all training sessions is mandatory. How can people learn the skills, change their behavior, learn how to step up to get things done, and learn to work together at a higher level if they are not present at the training?

So we make the training mandatory? Yes. I know that sounds crazy, so let me explain. Remember the Quality Circles of the late 1980's, where participation was voluntary? I always thought that was crazy because half the people didn't show up. Wow, don't your competitors love that! Then, when we figured out that wasn't any good, we made it mandatory and alienated everyone. So, I typically use the word "expected". Every person is expected to attend. That's nice, but people still tend to slip away. So I'm back to mandatory. Why, when making it mandatory could alienate people? Because a good trainer or coach can cut through that. The right person can draw people in and get them to "want" to get involved. Many times you do not have someone like that on staff. Use all the information in this book to choose someone wisely (more on this later). By taking attendance and publishing an up-to-date attendance matrix, we can close the back door until people make the transition. It helps leaders set an expectation with no wiggle room... that all the complaining about how Lean doesn't affect you, and how you don't have time, won't work. Anyone who then wants to exit after all that maybe should be allowed to exit (more on this later). If you want to sustain Lean, everyone, from the front to the back, even the owner, must attend all sessions. Everyone must see and hear the same thing.

We Must Work Together

Success in becoming the best in the world at what you do comes from not only working hard, but also doing the right things. True, but there is a critical element missing...how do you become the best if you do not work together effectively? Your success is not going to come from one person who creates something brilliant...although that certainly helps. Rather, your success will more than likely come from all the little things that everyone does, which when added together, become a huge thing that takes you to the top. Almost every process you can name involves several people from multiple functions. How do you achieve success if some are allowed to opt out? How do you achieve success when some are told, in effect, that they can go off on their own? That doesn't make sense! Working together means learning together. Every person must attend all training sessions together to learn to work together effectively.

Mix Them Up

When you select your groups for training, make sure you mix everyone up. Every group should have an office person, a production associate, an engineer, a maintenance person, a supervisor, a quality person, a member of senior management...well, you get it, right? I love the mix for these reasons:

- It assists with internal networking – it's always good to have lots of internal contacts when you have a problem or need to get something done.
- It helps people appreciate where someone else is coming from.
- It helps people appreciate what someone else is struggling with.
- It helps build relationships.
- It makes everyone human.
- It helps cement the concept, "we're all in this together".

It Takes Horsepower

I'm going to address this more in the next chapter, but just a word here – your transformation to becoming the best takes horsepower. This horsepower, or people power if you will, is the ability of people to get things done. How do you harness that horsepower if people have opted out…if they haven't involved themselves in the process?

Key People may Resist

I have found that in many organizations key people in leadership and support positions may also resist the Lean initiative. Some reasons:
- They take exception to someone invading their territory.

- They feel guilty that they haven't made the changes necessary, so they defend the current method.
- They feel like their power is being taken away.
- They take it as a personal attack.
- They created the current process. They take personal pride in it! There's no way there's a better method!
- They see it as a lack of respect for them and their position.
- They disagree with the direction.
- They'd love to see it fail to prove their point.
- Pride.
- They think someone is showing them up.
- They feel that other people are doing an "end around" around them.
- They won't give someone from the outside the credit.
- They see it as a lack of support for them.
- They feel management is putting them on the back burner. They are now on the outside looking in.

We need to help these people get past all this! Don't ignore it and don't let them slide...but be respectful.

Conclusion

It's crazy to expect Lean sustainability without involving every position, every job title, and every area. Improvements can and must be made in every area, which means that every person, every position, has critical changes to make.

Critical concepts learned in this chapter:
1. Every person, position, job title, and area, must be involved in the Lean process.
2. We must blur the lines. No one is better than anyone else.
3. We need perfect attendance at all training sessions.
4. We must have a good mix of people in each training session.
5. We must work together.
6. We must have every area making improvements.
7. We need to harness every bit of horsepower if we are to reach our goal of being the best in the world.
8. We must help people get past their resistance.

Got Lean? Law #3

Practice Exercise: Law #3

Complete the following and check your answers with the answer sheet found on page 104. Do not treat this as a test. The goal is not to get a high grade, but to get them all correct. If you don't know an answer, look back through the materials to find it.

1. Attendance at all training sessions must be:
    a. Mandatory.
    b. Voluntary.
    c. Expected.
    d. Done willingly and enthusiastically.

2. Key people may resist getting involved because:
    a. It's an invasion of their territory.
    b. Their pride gets in the way.
    c. They think they're being shown up.
    d. They won't give someone else the credit.
    e. All of the above.

3. Every person, in every area, have things that they alone must do. It's personal to them and their job. If they don't do it, who will?
    a. True.
    b. False.

4. Every person must be _____, no matter their job _____, how _____ they are, or what _____ they wear.

Got Lean? Law #3

5. How do you _____ horsepower if people have opted out.

6. A great way to sabotage positive change is to:
    a. Hire a consultant.
    b. Allow certain people to opt out of the training.
    c. Allow someone who doesn't know what they're doing to change it.
    d. Talk about touchy-feely stuff.
    e. B and C.

7. Mixing people from throughout the organization during training allows:
    a. The trading of recipes and showing pictures of the grandkids.
    b. Internal networking.
    c. Appreciation for other people.
    d. The building of relationships.
    e. B, C, and D.

8. Each person must be _____ involved in a process and it's improvement:
    a. Somewhat.
    b. Never.
    c. Appropriately.
    d. Actively.
    e. C and D.

Got Lean? Law #3

9. Too many times people struggle to be competitive using a _____ process.

10. Working together means _____ together.

Law #3: Lean Must Encompass Every Area

Self Assessment

No				Yes		
1	2	3	4	5	1)	Is every person, position, job title, and area involved in the Lean process?
1	2	3	4	5	2)	Have we blurred the lines – no one is better than anyone else?
1	2	3	4	5	3)	Do we have perfect attendance at our Lean training sessions?
1	2	3	4	5	4)	Do we have a good mix of people in each training group?
1	2	3	4	5	5)	Are people working together, no matter their job title, status, or what they wear?
1	2	3	4	5	6)	Is every area making improvements?
1	2	3	4	5	7)	Are we harnessing horsepower?
1	2	3	4	5	8)	Are we helping people get past their resistance?

Law #3: Lean Must Encompass Every Area

Group Discussion Questions

1. Given the self assessment questions on the previous page, what are your organization's:

    Strengths:

    Weaknesses:

2. What can you do to help people from each area get involved in the Lean process?

3. Why is it critical for everyone to attend every training session – to have perfect attendance?

4. What areas of our organization are actively involved in the Lean process? Which areas are not?

5. Why is it important to have every area engaged in the Lean process?

6. What methods are we using to get beyond the resistance of some? How effective are these methods? What else can we do?

Got Lean? Law #3

Practice Exercise Answer Sheet

1. A
2. E
3. A
4. Valued/respected, title, educated, clothes
5. Harness
6. B
7. E
8. E
9. Flawed
10. Learning

Law #4

Lean is a Way of Thinking

Law #4: Lean is a Way of Thinking

As you go through the Lean journey every person must learn to think differently. This way of thinking isn't easy. It takes time. There are many obstacles. Some of the critical components that assist in learning to think differently include:

- A person must have a desire to change their way of thinking.
- We need to define this new way of thinking.
- We need to become skilled in this way of thinking.
- We must overcome the obstacles to this way of thinking.
- We need to learn any helpful hints that will assist us in thinking differently.

Our theoretically perfect goal for "Law #4" is:

> Every person must learn the Lean way of thinking.

Once you get everyone involved and moving toward positive behavior, this new way of thinking is your next big obstacle. It could take several months to several years for people to make this transition.

You must be patient. Remember these people have decades of experience with the old way of thinking. It is very engrained. It has given us all the success we've had in the past. So people will not be easily convinced. You'll need all the leverage you can muster to change it.

Why the Need to Change

People need to realize that we must change. We don't have a choice! Why? Because of competition! With the competition we face today, if you do things the way you've always done them, you won't get what you always got... You'll get run over and put out of business by your competitors! We were successful in the past using our current methods, but we need to change our way of thinking if we are to be successful in the future. This "need to change" is no one's "fault", but rather the end product of a global market. It's not a personal attack on any person and the way they've done things! As Donald Trump likes to say, "*It's nothing personal, it's just business*".

Every Person Must Change

Critical to becoming the best is the expectation and requirement that every person must change. Each person must find that thing, or those things, that they must change...and change them!

Thinking in a New Way

Remember the book, "Quality: I'll know it when I see it?" The author makes the point that quality is difficult to define but he'd know it if he saw it! This "Lean way of thinking" is something like that. This way of thinking is easier to "see" than define.

While it's a little difficult to define, I'll make a stab at it. First, what I describe as the old way of thinking includes people doing things the way they've always been done because they've always done them that way. We've had success doing it! When someone tells people using the "old method of thinking" that they need to change, they:
- Rebel.
- Complain.
- Get defensive.
- Defend the current method.
- Take it as a personal attack.
- Attack the person who is introducing the change.
- Suck the energy out of everyone.
- Bend the ear of the highest level person they can get to listen.
- Create so much confusion, no one knows what's going on.
- Ignore the change.
- Do the change halfway.

- Comply if forced.

It's extremely difficult to make positive changes when the old way of thinking is practiced. While some people do accept change and incorporate it as best they can, the group that resists will typically waste everyone's time. They can and do hold us hostage. These seemingly wonderful people can turn into 30 percenter's real quick when you start talking about change.

The new way of thinking takes place when every person actively engages in the improvement process. They don't accept the current process as the only way to do something, or the best way to do it. They constantly ask the questions, "*What is the best way to do this? How can I improve this process? Where's the waste and how can I eliminate it?*" They are constantly trying to improve. They don't care who created the current process. They don't look back except to learn from history.

Patience, Control, and Chaos

Given our definition of the new way of thinking, some people see chaos. They claim that you can't be changing everything, all the time. They're right! You don't want to! So part of our definition has to include control. We must move forward patiently and in control. Contrary to popular belief, patience is not standing around hoping something happens. Patience means creating a plan and working that plan one action item at a time. You can't do everything all at once. That would indeed create chaos. Each person must do something every day to improve their process.

Learning to Think Differently

There are many classes on Lean that can help people to think differently. I can't cover all of those here. In fact, anything you can do to learn and help others learn, is well worth your effort. Discussions, reading books and magazine articles, and taking college and other training classes will help immensely. However, there are things you can do on the job, in addition to all of these things, which will help people learn to think differently. These include:

- Develop a flowchart of the process. This will uncover things that don't make sense or take too much time. Get people thinking of what works, what doesn't, and where the waste is hiding.

- Ask people what bugs them about a process. What drives them crazy? What are their pet peeves? I call these pet peeves "loose strings". Pull on any loose string because there is typically waste attached to it!

- Ask people what the effect of a change would be. I once had a group that didn't think setup reduction was possible. I asked them, *"But what if you "could" reduce setup time? What would the impact be?"* Once they realized the incredible potential impact, they began to rethink their position. They ended up cutting setup time in half.

- Examine your key measurables. Focus on improving delivery, quality, cost or some other critical area. Engaging people in this improvement process is teaching the new way of thinking.

- Create a pilot cell to focus attention. This process can then be duplicated once it's perfected. Remember, you can't do everything at one time.

Use every opportunity to develop a new way of thinking. Everything, from monthly plant wide meetings to one-on-one discussions can be used in this learning process.

Learn to See Waste

This new way of thinking involves the ability to see waste. The eight deadly wastes include:

1. **Overproduction/overproducing.**
Overproduction creates more than what we need, most times to compensate for problems in the system. Overproduction is the main reason for large inventory levels. Each person must identify when and why we overproduce. Typical reasons for overproduction in a manufacturing area include: To make up for scrap or rework, to cover for machine breakdowns, to account for supplier issues... In other words, "just in case". In the office, overproducing means producing more paper or information than is needed, or producing it early. Think about an order that is processed too soon. By the time it should have been processed, just-in-time, we've changed it several times. That creates the waste of overproducing. Measure it and challenge people to improve on it!

2. **Inventory.** "Any materials" (raw material, work in-process, assembly, or finished goods) in the system, anywhere in the organization. Help people understand the high price of inventory. In the office this includes excess supplies, copies, and office furniture.

3. **Conveyance.** Any transfer or transport for any reason of materials, paperwork, parts, assemblies, work in process or finished goods

from one location to another. This includes the movement of people. Measure and discuss how much distance materials or paperwork is moved and how much distance is required to find or deliver things. How do we reduce it?

4. **Defects/Correction.** Defect waste is made up of several layers. It includes the actual defects, but also the time and money spent on containing the problem with the customer, inspections or extra inspections, sorting, reworking, and repairing. It can include errors in paperwork, quotes, purchasing documents, HR documents, and other critical processes. One defect can create a cascading effect of waste.

5. **Processing Waste.** Processing waste occurs when you have process steps or operations that are not necessary and the customer will not pay for. Tumbling parts to remove burrs is an example in a manufacturing setting. Excessive reviews and multiple signatures are examples in the office.

6. **Operation/Motion Waste.** Operation waste occurs within the operation itself. It is waste associated with any movement that is not required to perform the operation. Help people measure and improve their cycle time – the time

it takes to perform their task. Eliminate any unnecessary walking, reaching, or bending. This is a great way to teach the new way of thinking.

7. **Idle Time/Waiting.** Idle time occurs when either a person and/or a machine waits, for any reason. This is not keeping people busy just to create more "work in process". This has to do with everyone using their time productively. In the office, idle time is created by waiting for signatures, emails, supplies, or other necessary items.

8. **Not Using the Talent of People.** Not using the talent of people occurs when people are not included in the improvement process, which means missed opportunities. This can result in everything from a lack of ideas to a reluctance to take ownership for making changes.

Theoretically Perfect Goals

Get people actively involved in making progress toward the following theoretically perfect goals:
- Production – zero changeovers.
- Quality – zero defects.
- Cost – zero waste.
- Delivery – zero late deliveries.

- Safety – zero injuries.
- Maintenance – zero breakdowns.
- Customer service – zero complaints.
- Financial performance – zero red ink.

Working toward these goals will create enough work to keep even the complainers engaged, if that's possible.

Overcome the Obstacles

There are many obstacles that stand in the way of the new way of thinking. They include:

Obstacle 1. Being held hostage. Our grizzled veterans have a way to hold us hostage. They control what gets done. They control our processes. They either create the process or do the hands-on-work. We learned in Laws #1 and #2 that we must take them with us. In addition to what we've talked about before, here are some additional thoughts that may help:
- Help them solve a pet peeve or fix something that makes their life easier. This can sometimes help draw them in.
- Ask lots of questions and gather lots of facts. Many times, what they're saying is accurate. Help them get past the barrier to make things better.
- Respect them. Develop the relationship.

- If you don't have the answer, admit it. Don't blow smoke at them.
- Ask for their help to solve a problem.

Obstacle 2. Assuming the process is perfect. There is always something that can be improved. Measure what's happening and challenge people to improve.

Obstacle 3. Trying to visualize it all at once. You must learn to divide and conquer. Many people like to throw every reason why something can't be done in your face to confuse and divert attention away from action. So nothing gets done because the details seem overwhelming. You must learn to divide it all into pieces and attack each item individually.

Obstacle 4. Assuming someone is a 30 percenter. Be careful that you really, truly understand where a 30 percenter is coming from. Sometimes a 30 percenter is really a frustrated 20 percenter. Listen by asking lots of questions to sort things out.

Obstacle 5. Making assumptions. Never assume. It will get you in deep trouble. Ask questions and gather facts. These are the basic tools of the new way of thinking.

Obstacle 6. Buying into the argument that says, "*If it ain't broke, don't fix it*". In reality, you will be constantly tweaking and playing with processes to find improvement. But you do need to learn to tweak at the right time so that you don't end up in chaos.

Getting Things Done Takes Horsepower

Lean thinking takes horsepower, or rather, people power. I look at horsepower as the ability to get things done. Horsepower is the driving force behind your Lean effort. You must tap into every available skill and turn whatever talent you see into skill.

I had a cell group of ten people once who couldn't get something fabricated because maintenance was buried with work. My question to them was, *"Why don't you fabricate it yourself?"* Here are the reasons they gave for not doing it themselves:
- It's not our job.
- Our supervisor won't let us.
- We don't have time.
- We don't know how.
- It still needs to be designed and sketched.

And when we found out that one of the people in the group had been a fabricator at a different company, we added one more excuse:
- We can't just let anybody do anything they want!

Are you kidding me? If you are worried about their skills, get them trained and certified. If you think you can't lose them while they do the job, act like they're on vacation and have people cover for them while they get it done.

My point? Use every skill, every talent, and every person to accomplish the task! Your future depends on it! Be creative! Respect that people will figure things out if challenged!

Do we need to learn stuff, build skills, and develop action plans to develop this horsepower? Absolutely! Now's the time to get going! Success favors an organization with lots of people who can get things done!

Bribery Works

I was explaining the concept of building relationships to a group to help them see that when you need something done by another person or department, it's an advantage to be able to go to someone who's a friend. A woman in class raised her hand and said, *"I've got that all figured out! I just bake cookies and brownies! I can pretty much get anything I need, when I need it!*

Everyone laughed, but when you think about it, that's the concept of building relationships to get things done. It is always beneficial to have a friend in your corner when you need help. Now I know that bribery does work!

Suggestion Systems Get You in Trouble

The foundation of most suggestion systems is the concept of listening to people and using their ideas. After all, they know more about their job than anyone else. We "want" to use their ideas. It's a way to show respect. It's the new way of thinking, right?

We then create a suggestion form for them to fill out and turn in. Here's the problem: creating the suggestion itself, is, in many cases, about one percent of the entire improvement process. Implementing the idea is the other 99 percent. So, we legitimize a process that allows, even encourages people, to do one percent of the work and hand it to someone else to do 99 percent of the work. And then, these same people who are doing one percent of the improvement work have the audacity to complain about the people doing 99 percent and how they're not getting enough done! And to top it off, when little or no action is taken by the people doing the 99 percent of the improvement work, these people doing 1 percent complain that no one is listening to them! Those people doing all the improvement work then become trapped doing a low priority, or meaningless task, simply because it was an approved suggestion. Can you see the problem here? This is extremely frustrating to everyone in the organization, both to those who feel they aren't being listened to, and to those burdened by all the work! This is definitely not the new way of thinking!

A better way to handle this is to have every person, team, department, and the organization develop lists of ideas, problems, improvements, and things that need to get done outside of the normal work load. These items can be passed to the person or group that has the responsibility and authority to get them done. Each person or group prioritizes their list and chooses one high priority item to complete. They develop objectives, action lists, responsibilities, and measure progress and results. In this way, every person is expected to contribute. This new way of thinking forces us to change our way of listening to people. We must listen, yes, but more than that, we need to empower and create a spirit of permission. We need to revamp our old suggestion systems. I don't care how many ideas a person comes up with... I care how many they implement!

Let me state the obvious here. If this new way of thinking demands the involvement of each person...then these same people will need to develop relationships, various technical skills, and the thinking necessary to implement improvements. We have a country full of people that can't do this! They've never been expected to! So we need to challenge them to learn...to step up. I have tremendous confidence that we can get this done, but it will take time, and people with great desire.

Be a Professional

Every person in the organization must learn to be a professional. Clean up the language, dress appropriately, change your attitude, act professionally, and step up to get things done.

Continue to Learn

Many of us think that learning is done when we finish school. Nothing could be farther from the truth. Each of us must embrace learning. We must be sponges. Learn all you can because the knowledge and skills you acquire become the fuel, or energy, for improvement. Many people and organizations have become stagnant because they've stopped learning. Your competitors love it when you stop learning!

We Can't Change Time, But We Can Change How We Use It.

While there is tremendous merit to reducing costs, people need to also understand the concept of "throughput". Throughput is the amount of output generated during a fixed amount of time. If you think about it, there is one constant that everyone faces... time. There are 60 minutes in an hour for every person. No one gets more, or less. What we can change, though, is how much output we generate in that time. If you reduce waste, eliminate unnecessary steps or processes, and make other positive changes, you can increase your throughput. Let's say you make those changes and you gain 50 percent more capacity. In other words, you can produce 50 percent more with the same people, equipment, and floor space. When you sell that capacity and produce more output, you're "sales" goes up by 50 percent, but at a reduced cost. This is where true improvements can be found! And they are available to everyone! We need to get busy pursuing these opportunities!

Elevate your Constraint

In any process is a constraint or bottleneck...some step or action that holds everything else up. In the office, it's the step that everyone stands around waiting for. On the plant floor, it's where the excess work in process accumulates. This constraint creates tons of waste. The best way to eliminate that waste is to discover, elevate, and reduce or eliminate the constraint or bottleneck. The new way of thinking demands that each person is skilled at doing this.

Note: Elevating a constraint means to shine a bright light on the constraint and attack it with everything you've got.

20-50-30 Rule Applied to Technical Skills

We have described the 20-50-30 rule as a measurement of someone's attitude. Let's change it a minute to describe the technical skills you find in your organization:

In a typical situation, 20 percent of the people have the technical skills to get the job done, whether it's bookkeeping or rocket science. They know all the ins and outs and details. If it's broke, they can fix it. If it needs to be improved, they know enough about how it works to figure it out. Another 50 percent are competent but are content to just keep things as they are. They are good at doing things the way they've always been done. While not going out of their way to improve things, they will help if asked. The remaining 30 percent either know enough to be dangerous or are changing things on their own when they have no business touching it. They mess things up more often then not, but yet don't seem to realize or won't admit they don't have a clue.

Look at the dynamics between the 20-50-30 attitude scale and the 20-50-30 technical skills scale. Remember, a 20 percenter on the attitude scale could be a 30 percenter on the technical skill scale. I've seen people who have a great attitude but no skills, and I've seen people with a terrible attitude that are as technically skilled as anyone you've ever met. The goal: Grow people to be 20 percenters on both the attitude and technical skills scales.

People must be Self-Managed

If a person has worked at a job for some period of time, like one year, five years, 20 years, and they still need to be told what to do...something's wrong! On one end of things, the reason might be that they have a supervisor who is extremely controlling...who doesn't allow a person to step up even if they have the skills to do it. This supervisor or manager makes all the decisions and you better not step out of line. These people need to get over themselves! They will fail because they can't possibly do it all themselves! On the other end of the spectrum, the reason why a person needs to be told what to do might be that they aren't stepping up, even though they may have all the skills

Got Lean? Law #4

necessary. Or, they don't have the skills and either don't know how to acquire them, or don't want to learn the skills necessary to step up. If these people don't change, they could put themselves in a position of being unemployable. No one will want them!

It might be helpful to look at the following illustration to understand the dynamics:

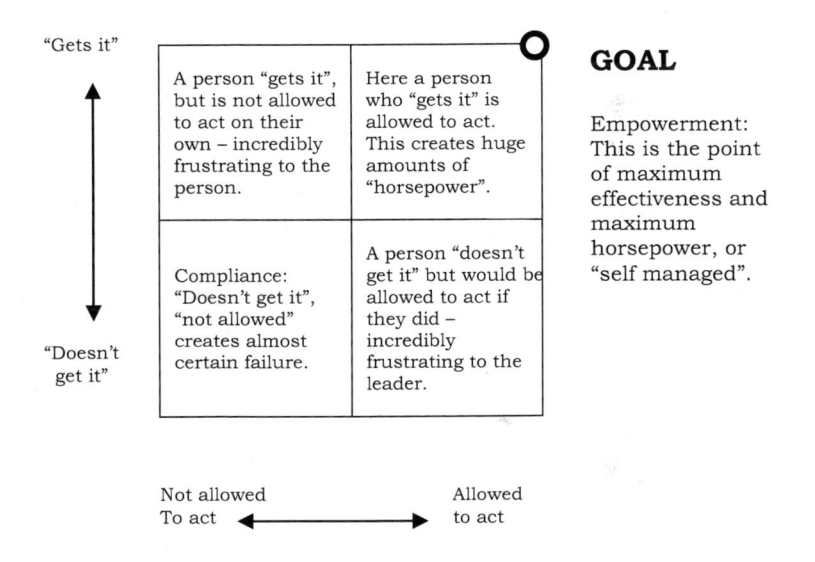

A person "gets it", but is not allowed to act on their own – incredibly frustrating to the person.	Here a person who "gets it" is allowed to act. This creates huge amounts of "horsepower".
Compliance: "Doesn't get it", "not allowed" creates almost certain failure.	A person "doesn't get it" but would be allowed to act if they did – incredibly frustrating to the leader.

Vertical axis: "Gets it" (top) ↕ "Doesn't get it" (bottom)

Horizontal axis: Not allowed To act ←→ Allowed to act

GOAL

Empowerment: This is the point of maximum effectiveness and maximum horsepower, or "self managed".

Notice in the lower left corner is a person who doesn't get it and would not be allowed to act anyway. This would be the area of compliance, which creates almost certain failure.

A person who "doesn't get it":
- Lacks attitude/desire.

- Lacks knowledge.
- Lacks skills.
- Doesn't own the objective.
- Doesn't use good judgment.

A person who "gets it":
- Has great passion/desire.
- Has great knowledge.
- Has great skills.
- Owns the objective.
- Gets things done.
- Uses good judgment.

Reasons for a leader who does not allow a person to act:
- Insecure.
- Control freak.
- Disrespectful.

Note: a person who "doesn't get it" must not be allowed to act.

Reasons for a leader who allows a person to act:
- Secure.
- Respects people.
- Doesn't need to micromanage.
- Realizes the great power of people.

Note: a person who "gets it" must be allowed to act.

As a person moves from "not getting it" to "getting it", the more freedom they must have to act. Their ability and authority to act must be proportional to how much they "get it".

Our goal is to assist people to reach the goal in the upper right hand corner, the point of "maximum effectiveness and maximum horsepower". The more a person "gets it" and the more they're allowed to act, the greater the effectiveness. In fact, when a person reaches the goal of "maximum effectiveness and maximum horsepower", they reach a point where they get things done at lightning speed without the need to be "managed". This is when you have reached true empowerment.

The days of just showing up for a job are over! The new way of thinking demands that each of us be self managed. We need the desire, knowledge, skills, tools and authority to manage ourselves. We need to allow people to act on their own. These are learned skills. But it takes time. It's also very different than what we're used to. We need to get past the reality that some people can't, and some people won't. Some leaders will allow you to act and some won't. Times a wasting. We better get it figured out!

Good Judgment

Wrapped around everything we've talked about, is the concept and skill of practicing good judgment. Good judgment means that we know when to back off and ask for help. It means we don't do things we're unfamiliar with. It is that little voice that tells you when something you're about to do is wrong, or will cause problems. It's the savvy that comes with experience and the caring that comes with a person who "gets it". Good judgment is another skill that can be learned.

Marketing vs. Selling

Producing something and then finding someone to buy it creates a lot of waste within any organization. That's called a sales approach. Many people do things because they think that's what people want them to do, or since we always did all this stuff, it must be important. How about this? Think about your job in terms of marketing...that's where you ask your internal customer what they need and you do just and only that. Shifting from a "sales" mentality to a "marketing" mentality will eliminate lots of waste.

Stop Doing It and See If Anyone Notices

There are many little kingdoms that have been created within organizations. These cause people to do tons of stuff that is meaningless or unnecessary. To find the waste, simply stop doing something and see if anyone notices. If no one notices, it may not be important. Be careful with this, though, because nothing is ever what it appears to be. In reality, gather facts before you stop doing something. Use good judgment.

Breeding Ground for 30 Percenters

The best breeding ground for 30 percenters is a situation where there is no challenge, no expectations, and no scoreboard. Create a visual scoreboard, set goals, and watch the 30 percenters dance! Eliminate the breeding ground and 30 percenters will have a tough time getting a foot hold. Kind of like eliminating standing water to rid yourself of mosquitoes.

Changing Habits

How do we get people to change their habits to embrace the new way of thinking? Challenge them, create a visual scoreboard, create a constant focus, create lots of repetition and continue to help them create desire. Help people work smart as well as hard.

Getting Traction

Getting traction in the new way of thinking can be helped by having each person choose a project and complete it. These projects should be small and they should be in the control of the person doing it. It helps affirm the need for everyone to step up and get involved.

Think "Perfect", not "Good enough".

Our theoretically perfect goal is to be the best in the world at what we do. That doesn't happen with a mindset of "good enough". Our goal is accomplished only through the single-minded pursuit of perfection and excellence. This pursuit of perfection must be the goal of every person.

Maintenance People must Change their Mindset.

Maintenance people often tell me their job is to fix things when they break. If that mindset isn't changed, nothing improves. We simply react to breakdowns, which means we are held hostage by them. Maintenance people should be like firefighters – they should spend the bulk of their time preventing breakdowns and a small portion of their time putting out fires, or fixing things. The theoretically perfect goal of a maintenance person should be "zero breakdowns."

By the way, all of us are maintenance people…think about it!

Anticipate What can Happen.

When do things break down? Yes, things break down when you least expect it and at the worst possible time. Your job is to anticipate what can go wrong. Kind of like an FMEA (Failure Modes and Effect analysis) for the entire process.

This means you must collect data and facts that assist you in "seeing" what's going on. This leads to anticipation and prevention. People who have learned the new way of thinking are good at these things.

Be like the Maytag Repairman.

What makes the Maytag repairman lonely? The machines don't break down! Why is that? Because everyone in the system, from design, to manufacturing, to shipping, is focused on the goal of reliability. Everyone must "get it" and be appropriately involved to reach this goal. This is a great example of our new way of thinking.

Technical Approach vs. People Approach

I advocate a people approach to sustaining Lean. But does that mean a technical approach can't work? Not at all! By technical, I mean "a group of technical people, like engineers, who use specific tools like Value Stream Mapping". I have encountered many organizations that have been successful with this technical approach. But in those same organizations, when I get a chance to apply a people approach, the results improve dramatically. It's true that technical people are not always good at the people side of things. They love the technical details and have a tendency to forget about people. Not intentionally – they're just trying to do their job. In fact, if you use the people approach, at some point, when everyone is moving in the right direction, your implementation plan must include this technical approach as well. It's just that when people "want to", they are much more willing to use the tools. So don't throw out all the technical stuff you've done – we'll need it. Just give people a chance to catch up. In many organizations, both the people approach and the technical approach can be applied concurrently.

Think Process not People

Many times, our first response to something going wrong or poor performance is to quickly blame people.

Maybe it's true that people are the problem in some cases, but I've found that if you think it's a people issue...it probably is not. It's more than likely a process issue. Improve the process and everyone becomes brilliant!

Outrun the "Foot"

Many people tell me that they are sick of the "foot in the middle of their back". This means that they are being pushed by management to make improvements. People must understand that with the intense competition of today, this "foot in the back" will not go away...unless you outrun it! In other words, make improvements that create results that outpace both your competition and your customers. Outrun the foot!

The Guy Called "They" Doesn't Exist

We've all heard this many times, *"They ought to..."* This is the ultimate copout and is used by many to shift responsibility to some unknown, undesignated person. Have you ever met this guy called "they"? He better show up pretty quick – he's got a lot of work to do!

For those of you waiting for this guy called "they" to show up, I've got some bad news for you! This person doesn't exist! This "they" thing provides evidence that some people would rather shift responsibility than take it!

Conclusion

The new way of thinking is difficult to achieve because we've never expected most people to use it. As a result, we have a country full of people who don't know how to get things done! We need to change that! The new way of thinking involves:
- Engaging everyone in the improvement process.
- Not accepting that the current process is the best way.
- Asking questions and gathering facts that probes for waste.
- A constant desire to improve and move toward perfection.

Critical concepts learned in this chapter:
1. We need to think in a new way.
2. Exercise patience and control to prevent chaos.
3. Learn to think differently.
4. Learn to see waste by examining the eight deadly wastes.
5. Develop actions to reach our theoretically perfect goals.
6. Overcome the obstacles.
7. Develop horsepower to get things done.

Got Lean? Law #4

8. Suggestion systems can get you in trouble.
9. Be a professional.
10. Continue to learn.
11. We can't change time, but we can change how we use it.
12. The 20-50-30 rule applied to technical skills can help us to further understand people.
13. People must learn to be self-managed.
14. Use a marketing approach versus a selling approach.
15. Sometimes we need to stop doing something and see if anyone notices.
16. Recognize the breeding ground for 30 percenters.
17. Changing habits is difficult to pull off.
18. Getting traction is necessary to begin the change process.
19. Think "perfect", not "good enough".
20. Maintenance people must change their mindset.
21. Anticipate what can happen.
22. Be like the Maytag repairman.
23. Understand both the technical approach and the people approach to Lean.
24. Think process, not people.
25. Outrun the "foot".
26. This guy called "they" doesn't exist.

Got Lean? Law #4

Practice Exercise: Law #4

Complete the following and check your answers with the answer sheet found on page 142. Do not treat this as a test. The goal is not to get a high grade, but to get them all correct. If you don't know an answer, look back through the materials to find it.

1. People who use the new way of thinking are good at:
    a. Knowing when something is good enough.
    b. Following orders.
    c. Reaching a standard.
    d. Anticipation and prevention.
    e. B and C.

2. Throughput is:
    a. The standard for a fixed period of time.
    b. The amount of output generated in a fixed amount of time.
    c. Sales generated in a variable amount of time.
    d. A fixed amount of output during any amount of time.

3. The transition to a new way of thinking happens quickly:
    a. True.
    b. False.

4. If you think you have a people issue, it probably isn't. More than likely it's a _____ issue.

Got Lean? | Law #4

5. "They" is a guy who:
   a. Better show up soon. He's got a lot of work to do.
   b. Is a way for people to shift responsibility.
   c. Is quite shadowy.
   d. Everyone knows, but has never seen.

6. The reason we must change is because of:
   a. Competition.
   b. Greedy business owners.
   c. Power hungry leaders.
   d. Politicians and NAFTA.
   e. B and D.

7. Loose strings are:
   a. Something to trip over.
   b. 30 percenters who should be fired.
   c. Pet peeves attached to waste.
   d. People who try to do things on their own.

8. The definition of "horsepower" is:
   a. Having to do with Clydesdales and beer.
   b. The ability to get things done.
   c. The ability of maintenance to keep up.
   d. Equates to how much a leader can get out of people.
   e. Only A – I didn't get past the beer!

9. Some of the biggest 30 percenters are our most _____ people.

Got Lean? Law #4

10. One of the best questions in the new way of thinking, is:
    a. Who's to blame and how can I make them feel pain?
    b. How much more money are you offering?
    c. How much success have we had doing it the current way?
    d. What's the best way to do this?

11. The new way of thinking is accomplished through the single minded pursuit of _____ and _____.

12. We can get held hostage by:
    a. Grizzled veterans.
    b. 30 percenters.
    c. Support people.
    d. People in a formal leadership position.
    e. All of the above.

13. Bribery works.
    a. True.
    b. False.

14. The fuel and energy for improvement comes from:
    a. High energy drinks.
    b. Red Kool-Aid and red Jell-O.
    c. Constant and continual learning.
    d. Effective leadership.
    e. The 50 percenters.

Got Lean?   Law #4

15. Good judgment is the _____ that comes with experience and the _____ that comes with a person who gets it.

16. We are all maintenance people.
    a. True.
    b. False.

17. The point of maximum effectiveness and maximum horsepower happens when:
    a. A person who doesn't get it is allowed to act.
    b. A person who doesn't get it is not allowed to act.
    c. A person who gets it is allowed to act.
    d. A person who gets it is not allowed to act.
    e. What?

18. Suggestion systems must be changed to:
    a. Group studies.
    b. Everyone is doing what they want, when they want to.
    c. Meetings to better prioritize ideas.
    d. Implementation systems.
    e. People checking their brains at the door.

19. The new way of thinking is hampered by:
    a. People who don't want to.
    b. People who can't.
    c. Leaders who won't allow you to act.
    d. Leaders who don't know how to empower.
    e. All of the above.

Law #4: Lean is a Way of Thinking

Self Assessment

No				Yes		
1	2	3	4	5	1)	Are people thinking in a new way?
1	2	3	4	5	2)	Do we exercise patience and control?
1	2	3	4	5	3)	Are people learning to think in a new way?
1	2	3	4	5	4)	Are we seeing and attacking waste?
1	2	3	4	5	5)	Are we using the horsepower available to us?
1	2	3	4	5	6)	Does our suggestion system reward implementation?
1	2	3	4	5	7)	Are people behaving professionally?
1	2	3	4	5	8)	Are we a learning organization?
1	2	3	4	5	9)	Are we focusing on throughput?
1	2	3	4	5	10)	Are our people becoming self managed?
1	2	3	4	5	11)	Are we applying strategies to create traction in the new way of thinking?
1	2	3	4	5	12)	Are we thinking "perfect" not "good enough"?
1	2	3	4	5	13)	Are the maintenance people changing their mindset?
1	2	3	4	5	14)	Are we anticipating what could happen?
1	2	3	4	5	15)	Are we being like the Maytag repairmen?
1	2	3	4	5	16)	Are we thinking process not people?
1	2	3	4	5	17)	Are we successfully outrunning the foot?
1	2	3	4	5	18)	Have we thrown out this guy called "they"?

Law #4: Lean is a Way of Thinking

Group Discussion Questions

1. Given the self assessment questions on the previous page, what are your organization's:

    Strengths:

    Weaknesses:

2. What are you doing to help people become self managed?

3. Why is it critical for people to continue to learn?

4. Why is horsepower important?

5. What methods of horsepower are we using? What methods are we missing?

6. Do our people get things done? What things have been implemented in the last month?

7. What happens if our people don't learn to think differently?

Got Lean? Law #4

Practice Exercise Answer Sheet

1. D
2. B
3. B
4. Process
5. B
6. A
7. C
8. B
9. Skilled
10. D
11. Perfection, excellence
12. E
13. A
14. C
15. Savvy, caring
16. A
17. C
18. D
19. E

Law #5

Lean Focuses on Results, Not Activities

Law #5: Lean Focuses on Results, not Activities

Many people and organizations are so worried about using a specific Lean tool or making sure everyone is busy that they forget to focus on results. Running around like a chicken with your head cut off, having hundreds of action items, and focusing on "activity", doesn't accomplish much if your results don't improve. Everything you do must improve results. Don't look at what a person says or does, look at and measure what they accomplish!

Our theoretically perfect goal for "Law #5" is:

> Use scoreboards to measure and make visual what's important.

The technical term for this process is Lean Metrics, Key Performance Indicators, or Scoreboards, as I like to call them.

Lean Metrics Defined

Lean Metrics refers to the method of keeping score of process improvements and on-going performance. Some of the critical reasons for keeping score include:
- To track performance to goals.
- To create ownership for improvements.
- To compare improvement results with old practices.

- To create leverage to convince doubters that the new method is better.
- To set goals.
- To create an in-depth understanding of how a process/system is operating.
- To create energy for the team responsible for the improvements.
- To create a foundation of factual data with which to make decisions.
- To create and sustain momentum.

Keeping score is a foundational element within your organizational infrastructure. It is also crucial to Lean sustainability. It allows you to monitor critical elements of your performance, respond appropriately to changing conditions, and set and achieve goals that assist you in becoming the best in the world at what you do.

Lean Metrics and Empowerment

You must practice "Empowerment" if you are going to be successful in today's global economy. My definition of empowerment:

> Creating an environment in which people want to,
> and do, take ownership for results.

The primary focus of every leader is to create this environment. A major element in creating the environment is keeping score. In my work with many different organizations, I consistently see a lack of focus. I believe this is because there is not an effective scoreboard in place. It's like everyone is playing the game, but only the owner of the team knows the real score. Sometimes, even the coach doesn't know the score.

For example, in one company recently, the owner kept telling the tool room manager that the tool room was losing money. This manager was dumb-founded because they were busy all the time. *"How can we be losing money?"* he repeated over and over again. Nothing changed until the manager was given access to the numbers. Only then could he effectively contribute to turning the situation around.

In the great majority of cases, though, it's hourly people who are not focused. They not only don't see a scoreboard, they don't even know how the game is played! This information is kept from them. Many companies are still run the old fashioned way. They hire people and ask them to check their brain at the door. They're told *"just do what you're told. You don't have to worry about anything else"*.

I strongly disagree with this style. If you want to be the best, you need "all hands on deck". If you keep your hourly people in the dark, it's like having the coach yell out every move each player needs to make before they can make it. How many games do you think you'll win? Many people are playing the game but have no idea what the score is.

My belief and passion is that every person in the organization must understand how the business operates. Every person must be involved in improving the processes they come in contact with. Every person must be able to "see" the scoreboard. This creates the environment within which people will take ownership for results.

It's tough to expect people to get excited about, or own, something they know little about. Your job is to create a scoreboard that is appropriate to the organization, department, team or person/position.

I know! You're saying that you do have a scoreboard! But, is it personal to the person, or does it only measure corporate results? Can each person "see" the scoreboard and is it personal to them?

Greatest Obstacles

When I first walk into an organization I find one of four things is happening: (1) there are no measurements in place, or (2) there are some measurements but they are not visual, or (3) there are so many that they've become distracting and confusing, or (4) only a corporate scoreboard is used. Let's look at each of these:

1. **No measurements** - this occurs when only a select few people see the numbers. Some reasons for this include:
    - The owner thinks people will share them with competitors.
    - People in charge think its nobody else's business.
    - Management thinks people won't understand them.
    - Management thinks people will misinterpret them.
    - Everyone's too busy to think about it.
    - There is a group that loves to "control" information.
    - Some people use it as "leverage" or "power".

2. **Some measurements, but not visual** – this occurs when there are some sporadic

measurements available for some areas, but they are not visual. Some reasons for this include:
- People don't realize the power and impact behind making the score visual.
- It's not easy to make it visual.
- We're too busy to take the time to get it done.
- We think it's visual, but it's not.

3. **Too many measurements** – this happens when the scoreboard has so many charts, it's difficult to focus. This happens because:
   - If one chart is good, fifty are better.
   - An inability to focus and prioritize.
   - Too much attention to detail.
   - Thinking that everyone needs every score.
   - Thinking that every chart must be displayed.

4. **Only a corporate scoreboard is used** – there is nothing wrong with having a corporate scoreboard, but it does not create personal ownership within each person in the organization.

Scoreboard Obstacles

Within all of the things I've mentioned, here are several key points that I'd like to address. I feel these are the greatest obstacles to creating a scoreboard:

- **Reluctance to share the numbers** – for whatever the reason, whether you feel it's nobody's business, you think people will share the data with your competitors, or you think they won't understand...whatever the reason...you need to get beyond it. Working without a scoreboard is like driving a car blindfolded, with the person next to you telling you the moves to make. This might be a lot of fun to watch, but it's no way to run a business. Every person needs instant visual information in order to make second by second decisions critical to their success.
  Here are some helpful guidelines:
    - Start with simple and non-threatening charts like on-time delivery or safety.
    - Slowly add measurements and charts that affect the success of the organization, department, team, and position.
    - Educate people over time. Don't back up the truck and dump everything on them at once. Roll it out one item at a time

and explain how it works and what it does.
- **Problems with control or power** – these people are on power trips. If you are one of these, you need to get over yourself. While this is a bigger subject than we have room for, here are some suggestions:
    - Find a mentor that can hold you accountable for making necessary changes to your style.
    - Find a coach who can teach you how to empower people.
    - Examine whether you have the knowledge and skills to lead. If not, get them.
    - Remember that leading by fear or control will lead to eventual failure.
- **Too much detail** – the trick to improving operations is to simplify things. You must concentrate on the few important items and set aside the dozens of little things that consume your time and prevent you from doing things critical to your success. When things get tough, some of us dive into the details and drive everyone out of their minds. Remember, this will freeze everyone up! You must simplify, at least in the short term. Some ideas:
    - List your key measures and focus on them.

- Prioritize, and work on the highest priority.
- Start with improving processes that affect your key measurables.
- Leverage your efforts by focusing on those things that will solve several problems with one action.
- Involve people in the key measurables that they have control over, rather than dumping all measurables on them.

- **Not visual or personal enough** – remember each person must see the scoreboard. You don't play the game in the gym and either not keep score or have the scoreboard located somewhere else.
    - Create scoreboards in each work cell or area that are personal to the person or team, in addition to departmental and corporate boards.
    - Make the data collection sheets and charts easy to fill out and update.
    - Expect each person or team to create, update, and maintain their own scoreboard.

Want to Improve? You Gotta Keep Score!

Improve a process – where do you start? The first stage of improving a process is to keep score. You do this by measuring where you are now. You must have a scoreboard if you hope to improve – how do you know if something is improving if you're not measuring it? Remember the old saying, *"What gets measured gets done!"* So if it's important, you better be measuring it. If you are not measuring it, and don't really want to, then it must not be important! Measuring something sends a message to everyone in your organization about what's important.

For example, how many people would show up for a high school basketball game if no one kept score? Some people say that only the parents would show up, but I think that's incorrect. Without a scoreboard, I don't think anyone would show up, not even the players. The scoreboard shows you what's important, how you're doing, and creates energy! The *"score"* must always be visual to the person doing the job. Don't play the game in the "gym" and keep score in the "cafeteria". Corporate scores are fine if they are found in the cafeteria, but each person needs a personal or team scoreboard that is visual to them at all times!

Measurements, Start to Finish

When you "measure" your process, you must define the parameters that define when the "clock" starts and ends.

If the start and stop times vary or are inconsistent, you won't be able to see what's happening in your process with any clarity. Parameters are necessary so that you can see the impact of your changes and/or improvements. You start and end at a consistent place each time.

The first time you measure you are simply trying to establish a baseline. There is no need to do anything special or different, just do your job! No need to cheat the system by fudging the numbers, skipping steps, or doing an *"easy"* version to look good! No need to force more beads of sweat on your forehead. (In other words, there is no need to work harder than you normally do, unless you typically don't work very hard). Just do what you do. Just do your job!

Assume that you've measured your results in a specific area for the first time. How do you think you did? In reality, you won't know how you did because you have nothing to relate it to, or with. Where you start isn't important – it's where you take it that counts. The first measurement tells you where you are today. Its history and no one can go back and change history. However, what does your "gut" tell you about how you did? Chances are that you and the group will say, "We can do better." Murphy's Law says that your first measurement will point out that you've got problems – you won't like what you see.

Additional Thoughts:

- The results of your first measurement don't matter. It's simply a starting point. Many people, especially people in leadership positions, get all worked up about the first set of numbers. Make sure you use your energy to improve, not to cry about what's past.

- The most important consideration/question is "Where can I take this?" and "What can I do to improve the process?"

- The two critical factors that must be managed if we are going to improve:

    1. Knowledge and skill of the people.
    2. The difficulty of the job.

Every job has a different difficulty level and every person has different knowledge and skills.

Try not to get caught up in simply putting the most skilled people on the most difficult jobs. That's a great place to start, it gets the job done, but two nasty things could appear:

1. No one else learns the job.

2. You could burn the person out.

Continually improving the process to reduce the difficulty will simplify the job and make it possible for anyone to do the job.

Set Goals

This is not a primer on setting goals, but we have to discuss them because they are critically important to your success. Here are a few thoughts on goals:

- People will not be skilled at setting goals at first. That's ok. Don't let that stop you. Get people involved in setting goals so they gain experience.

- Start with a 50 percent improvement goal, even though it seems disrespectful to set the goal that high to begin with. It seems like you're telling the people doing the job that they aren't very good at it. But in reality, you will typically see a 25 percent to 50 percent gain when you begin – this is called "low hanging fruit". This initial goal is not meant to be a personal attack.

- Don't argue or spend lots of time on the goal. "Setting" the goal is not the goal. The goal is to improve. I've seen people waste lots of time on the goal. Pick one that everyone can agree with and get to work. A question for anyone taking too long to set a goal – "How long are you going to discuss it before you pick one and get started?"

- Many times you don't get to set the goal – the customer sets it for you. You may not like this goal, but it is what the customer says it is. Help people understand this.

- If the goal is very aggressive (perhaps a goal set by the customer) you may not be able to reach it with your current process. This forces change because you'll need to look at how you do the job with a different set of eyes.

- Be careful to set a goal that is challenging, but attainable. People get demoralized if you set the goal too high. For example, if you have $150,000 per month of scrap, it would be rather ridiculous to set a goal of zero. We know that "0" is the ultimate, theoretically perfect goal, but setting a more reasonable goal of $75,000 per month would be a good place to start. Once you hit that goal, you can always raise or lower it to achieve more improvement.

- Use goals, not standards. Standards are important, but people doing the job will slack off when they hit the standard, or, the work available expands into the time available. You don't want this. Set goals that are a challenge to meet. These goals may, or may not, have something to do with the "standard".

Comments:

- Don't add people – improve the process.

- Your experts "may" have the toughest time with the improvements. We're asking them to do something different from what has made them successful. Any changes are met with, *"that's not the way you do it"*.

    - We depend on the expert.
    - We love the expert.
    - We sometimes have to do things different than what's been done before.
    - That irritates the expert.

    If you are going to be successful with lean, you must have full backing and involvement from your experts! They must own the improvement process!

- Your vision for innovating the process may be blocked by your past success.

- Chances are you won't reach the goal if you do it the way you've always done it. In many cases, you must look at your job from a completely different perspective. Ask yourself, *"What is the best way to do this job?"*

Process Fixation

Sometimes the "process" or "the way we've done something for a long time," becomes the "goal". It's important to realize that the "process" must never be the goal. This happens often with ISO requirements. People think that once they document a process, it can't be changed. That is wrong! The concept behind ISO is the same as the reason we measure something. How do you improve a process if you haven't documented what you do now? Again, the process is not the goal. The goal is always a number like scrap, parts produced, on-time delivery, efficiency, safety, etc. The "process" is actually the action plan to reach the goal. When you concentrate on the goal, the "process" becomes expendable and changeable.

In any job, the goal is to improve a key measurable – that makes the process itself negotiable. We don't necessarily care what the process is as long as we reach our goal. The only exception comes if/when we abandon our values or ethics for the "goal". Never do that!

So it's critical that you have a scoreboard that is visual to everyone. Each person must see where we are in relation to the goal. When the score is visual to everyone, the process is open to change. When the scoreboard is not visual, the tendency is for the process to become the goal, which leads to process fixation and a lack of desire to change. You show me a group that is unfocused and negative and I'll show you a group that is not challenged. Scoreboards provide that challenge and create energy.

Helpful Hints on Creating a Scoreboard

There are a number of things to keep in mind as you begin creating a scoreboard for any area. It takes a tremendous effort over a long period of time to create and maintain a scoreboard that effectively measures where you are at any given time. Some things to keep in mind:

- **Measure what's important** – measuring takes time, so you want to focus your efforts on what makes most sense. Ask, *"If I am the best in the world at this, how do I know?"* Generally, you want to focus on three elements:
    - Inputs – measure supplier effectiveness in the areas of quality, cost, delivery, response time, etc.

- Process – measures internal efficiency like cost, cycle times, labor costs, setup time, absenteeism, safety, etc.
- Outputs – measures your effectiveness in meeting your customers' requirements like on-time delivery, sell price, quality, etc.

Look back at our specific objective of "producing quality product or service, on time, at the least possible cost, in a safe manner, and have fun doing it". Measure these to begin with.

- **Keep it simple** – start out with a few simple measurements and build from there.

- **Observe before doing** – before doing anything, observe what people are doing. This will tell you a lot about what's important and what's not. Also, observing someone performing a task will help you begin to understand how to measure what they're doing.

- **Anything can be measured** – many people claim that you can't measure what they do. In fact, anything can be measured. Consider an example of a fuzzy objective: Good phone service. This can be broken down into several objective measurements:
    1. Answered on the first ring.

2. Talked with a smile on his/her face.
3. Warmly greeted the caller by name.
4. Asked the caller's name and reason for calling.
5. Asked appropriate questions to determine details.
6. Gave specific information on resolution or further contacts.
7. Thanked the person by name.
8. Wished them a good day at close of call.

As you can see, anything can be measured!

- **Recognize the difference between variable and attribute data** – there is a difference between data. Variable data occurs when you can count or measure in specific numbers. This occurs when you count the number of accidents or the number of late deliveries. You get a real number.

Attribute data occurs when you don't get a real number. It happens most often when you must determine Go/No Go or Yes/No type situations. Attribute data can also be turned into variable data. For example, people attending a party are either male or female – an attribute. But when you do the math, you find out that 67 percent of attendees were female – you then have variable data.

- **Data collection sheets must be simple and easy to fill out** – the foundation of any process improvement or problem solving process are facts. These facts must be gathered and compiled in the most simple and straight-forward way possible. Data collection sheets that are complex and time-consuming will probably not be used. Or at least the data will be incomplete, and therefore unusable.

The simpler a data collection sheet is and the easier it is to use, the greater the chance that people will actually collect the data.

So what makes an effective data collection sheet? Here are some guidelines:
- They are simple and easy to use.
- They gather basic facts only, not every conceivable fact.
- They are organized on preferably one page – the more pages, the more confusing.
- General rule of thumb is to list all of the main categories and break them down only once – this keeps you from trying to collect too much information.
- Break down each category more than once only if it is practical and easy to do.

- Each category must be measurable (a category like "bad eraser" is confusing – what does that mean?)
- Create categories before collecting data so everyone collects data consistently.

- **Involve people on a regular basis** – as much as possible, people must collect their own data and update their own charts. They should also be involved in setting goals. Weekly or monthly team meetings at the scoreboard(s) are also a must if people are to step up to improve their own performance.

- **Make your chart easy to read:**
    - Use a two dimensional bar graph – it's easiest to read.
    - Only one item per graph – too many lines, bars, or stacked bars make the graph difficult, confusing, and perhaps unreadable.
    - Make each graph consistent with the others in terms of how it looks and the numbers on the axis (vertical and horizontal) if possible.

- **Remember who reads your charts** - I am very persnickety about graphs. The person reading your graphs can be called your "customer". Your customer is the person in the trenches who must understand what the scoreboard is telling them in a split second. They don't have time to stand and read a chart. They're tied to a machine or line – they simply don't have time to try to decipher your graph. Your customer is not the person who reads charts every day. Remember, if your chart is too busy or crowded and can't be read easily, then it probably won't be read.

- **Scoreboards should be placed in the "working" area of the person doing the job -** If you don't agree, consider this: Go to the nearest high school and before a big basketball game, move the scoreboard from the gym to the cafeteria. See how long that lasts. It makes no sense to play the game in the gym and have the scoreboard hanging in the cafeteria.

Conclusion

Keeping score is crucial to focusing on results, not activity. It creates energy and momentum for becoming more competitive. It helps people own the improvement process. Every person must be able to see the scoreboard so that they can make minute to minute decisions. Keeping score also prevents process fixation, where the process becomes the goal. Scoreboards challenge people to step up to become the best in the world.

Critical concepts learned in this chapter:
1. Lean must focus on results, not activity.
2. Lean metrics help empower people.
3. We must overcome the obstacles, like "no measurements", "not visual", "too many measurements", or "having only corporate scoreboards."
4. We need to overcome our reluctance to share numbers.
5. We must set goals to challenge people.
6. We must measure what's important.
7. Anything can be measured.
8. People should collect their own data and create their own charts.
9. Make charts simple and consistent for easy comprehension.
10. Scoreboards should be personal and visual to the person doing the job.
11. Eliminate process fixation by using scoreboards that are personal to each person or team.

Practice Exercise: Law #5

Complete the following and check your answers with the answer sheet found on page 172. Do not treat this as a test. The goal is not to get a high grade, but to get them all correct. If you don't know an answer, look back through the materials to find it.

1. When you set a goal, start with:
    a. A 50 percent improvement.
    b. A goal that satisfies your customer.
    c. A goal that is challenging, not demoralizing.
    d. The standard – those are usually accurate.
    e. A, B, and C depending on the situation.

2. A major element in "creating the environment" is:
    a. Making sure everyone is intimidated.
    b. Keeping everyone happy.
    c. Keeping score.
    d. Creating fear.
    e. Buying donuts.

3. What gets _____ gets done.

4. Scoreboards can create _____ to convince a doubter that the new method works.

Got Lean? Law #5

5. The scoreboard must:
    a. Be visual to each person.
    b. Be hung in the cafeteria.
    c. Contain every possible chart.
    d. Include every detail.
    e. Include the horseshoe tournament results from the company picnic.

6. Scoreboards should be created that are personal to each person or team and:
    a. Allow ridicule and trash talking by others.
    b. Be updated and maintained by the person or team.
    c. Be used to "write a person up" when necessary.
    d. Be used to compare performance with others.

7. The most important question when creating a new chart is:
    a. Who's responsible and how can we punish them?
    b. What tool can I use?
    c. How can I blame it on someone else?
    d. Where can I take this? How can I improve?
    e. B and D.

8. Many times when a chart is first posted:
    a. No one believes it.
    b. Murphy's Law says it will look really bad.
    c. It shows that people cheated to make it look good.
    d. Someone in a formal leadership position freaks out.
    e. B and D.

9. Process fixation occurs:
    a. When the process becomes the goal.
    b. When any person fixes a process.
    c. When a scoreboard is used.
    d. When someone doesn't care what process is used.
    e. When an organization focuses on processes, not people.

10. Given a choice, what do you do?
    a. Throw people at the problem.
    b. Improve your process.
    c. Blame someone else.
    d. Shift responsibility to someone else.
    e. A, C, and D, depending on the situation.

11. The chart that is probably the easiest to read is:
    a. Pie chart.
    b. Line graph.
    c. 3d bar graph.
    d. 2d bar graph.
    e. Any graph is Ok.

Law #5: Lean Focuses on Results, Not Activities

Self Assessment

No				Yes		
1	2	3	4	5	1)	Are we focusing on results, not activity?
1	2	3	4	5	2)	Are we using Lean metrics to help empower people?
1	2	3	4	5	3)	Have we overcome the obstacles, like "no measurements", "not visual", "too many measurements", and "using only corporate scoreboards"?
1	2	3	4	5	4)	Are we sharing numbers?
1	2	3	4	5	5)	Are we setting goals, not standards?
1	2	3	4	5	6)	Are we measuring what's important?
1	2	3	4	5	7)	Is every job being measured?
1	2	3	4	5	8)	Are people collecting their own data and creating their own charts?
1	2	3	4	5	9)	Are charts simple and consistent for easy comprehension?
1	2	3	4	5	10)	Are scoreboards personal and visual to the person doing the job?

Law #5: Lean Focuses on Results, Not Activities

Group Discussion Questions

1. Given the self assessment questions on the previous page, what are your organization's:

    Strengths:

    Weaknesses:

2. What are the important things measured in your organization? Do you have a scoreboard to make the score visible to everyone?

3. Do your "experts" own the process of improvement? Why, or why not?

4. Has your "process" or "the way you do something" become the goal? Identify and describe examples of this.

5. Are scoreboards personal and visual to the person doing the job?

6. Are you focusing on results, not activity?

Got Lean? Law #5

Practice Exercise Answer Sheet

1. E
2. C
3. Measured
4. Leverage
5. A
6. B
7. D
8. E
9. A
10. B
11. D

Law #6
Lean is a Set of Tools, or Methods, for Finding and Eliminating Waste

Law #6: Lean is a Set of Tools, or Methods, for Finding and Eliminating Waste

The quick definition of Lean is: "to identify and eliminate waste". There are many tools that will help you accomplish this objective. This section will not be a primer on the use of the tools. I wouldn't have enough space. Rather, I want to give you a heads up on how and when to use some of the more popular tools.

These tools are progressive, in that to start with, you only need some simple tools to begin to identify and eliminate waste. After the low hanging fruit is gone, you'll need to turn to more sophisticated tools to get more specific and detailed information to develop simpler processes.

Our theoretically perfect goal for "Law #6" is:

> Use a tool that is appropriate to the situation

Build a House with a Hammer?

Would you ever build a house with just a hammer? Of course not! That's crazy! In fact, a carpenter brings an entire truck full of tools to the job site. This person is skilled in the use of each tool and knows exactly when to use it. And yet, many organizations rely on only a few tools, sometimes only one. In the early days of Lean, Kaizen Events were the poster child for Lean. Now, it's Value Stream Mapping. I'm not sure why people fixate on one tool like this. Maybe they think these tools are magic, or it's the latest rage...everyone's using it, so they need to be in the "in" crowd. The tools of Lean are not magic. In fact, as a person who "gets it" once said to me: *"I'm surrounded by waste! I don't need no stinkin tools! At least not yet!"*

I'm not saying these new tools are bad. They're not. Each of them is extremely valuable. But it seems like the most effective approach is to use the best tool for the situation. The mistake many people make is to think that Lean means "use a tool". The goal of Lean is to eliminate waste to improve performance, not to use a specific tool. The tool itself is used to assist in reaching the goal, it is not the goal itself.

Start Simply

If we are going to sustain Lean, it seems that we should start with the easier tools and migrate to the more difficult over time. Now, if you're thinking that you might miss something critical...don't. You can capture 80 percent of the same ideas using simple tools...ideas that you would need to implement first anyway, even if you had used a more sophisticated tool right away. This is called "picking the low hanging fruit", because it's easy to get. You don't need a sophisticated tool for that. And you won't confuse people in the process.

Dancing to the Oldies

Once the Lean tools were introduced, people seemed to give up on those they were using. These "oldies" were put out to pasture or thrown on the scrap heap. This is a mistake because these tools can be very valuable in certain situations. Does a carpenter throw out the traditional hammer after buying a pneumatic hammer? Did you throw out your circular saw when you purchased your table saw? Did you throw out your traditional stove when you bought a microwave? Did you throw out your garden hose when you bought a power washer? Sorry, I got a little carried away there! You get the picture, right? Some examples:

- Flow charting a process is a simpler, easier method that captures 80 percent or more of the improvements that a Value Stream Map would. It's a great way to lead into the Value Stream Map without adding immediate confusion. Follow it with a detailed Value Stream Map, or, better yet, parallel the two.
- Video tape a setup and identify areas for improvement before going into a full blown SMED process (Single Minute Exchange of Dies).

Got Lean?   Law #6

- Use Pareto Analysis to identify focus areas before doing a Kaizen Event.
- Ask lots of questions and gather basic facts before initiating any other kind of tool. This can uncover many areas of low hanging fruit.

These "oldies" can be highly effective in the hands of people who "get it".

Why We Fail

Most of the reason we fail in the use of the tools lies in the prep work. Does a farmer sow seed in a field without first preparing the soil? He wouldn't get much of a crop if he did! This book has detailed the prep work needed to get Lean to stick. I think, in reality, if the prep work is done correctly and you have a group of people who "get it", you can throw any tool at them and they'll eat it up. So it's not the tools that are the problem. The issue lies in when we throw a tool at them before they "get it". That's a disaster waiting to happen!

I find too many people, from both the office and the floor, who want to argue about whether the tool they've been taught works, or not, in their area. Helpful tip: when someone is arguing that the tool they've been taught doesn't work in their area, it's a sure bet that they don't "get it". Why? Because every tool, or at least the concept, can be used anywhere. People who "get it" are hungry for "anything" that can help! The final measurement as to whether someone gets it? Are they eliminating waste, or is it business as usual? A person who "gets it" works past obstacles. A person who doesn't get it simply finds excuses!

The Tools of Lean

The tools of Lean make perfect sense and are really cool when you thoroughly understand them. As we've said before, Lean is about common sense. Lean doesn't force us to do foolish things. So let's look at some of the tools. I have not covered them in detail, but give you enough information to understand them. I've also added some of my own personal twists that make them more effective.

The tools I'll cover include:
- 5S.
- Kaizen.
- Value Stream Mapping.
- SMED (Singe Minute Exchange of Dies).
- TPM (Total Productive Maintenance).
- Kanban.
- Pareto Analysis.
- 5W's and an H.

There are many more which I do not cover in this book.

Got Lean? Law #6

Tool Matrix

Tool	Use	Difficulty	Things to look out for
5S	- Good entry tool - Gets everyone involved - Anyone can do it	Easy	- Don't let it focus on cleaning and daily drudgery
Kaizen Event	- Needs to be led - Facilitator is critical - Gets results fast	Moderate/ Tough	- Don't allow too much homework
Value Stream Mapping	- Based on facts - Very detailed - Can "see" the process - Highly effective at improving entire process	Tough	- People tend to get blown away at first - Too much detail, too soon
SMED	- Get quick improvements in setup time - No difficult concepts to learn	Easy	- Start with video taping the setup and internal/ External discussions to create improvements
TPM	- Gets everyone involved - Shifts responsibility to entire organization	Easy/ Moderate	- TPM is not just for maintenance
Kanban	- Links entire process - Reduces inventory - Easy to visualize	Easy/ Moderate	- Start with a simple process and grow it
Pareto Analysis	- Based on facts - Is visual - Identifies priorities - Creates focus	Easy	- Make your data collection sheets simple
5W's and an H	- Creates respect - Earns trust - Digs for facts - Focuses attention - Seeks first to understand	Moderate	- This is more difficult than it should be because people are too judgmental

5S

A good tool to use as a starting point for lean thinking is 5S. These five actions are the support system for improvement in your company. This process is called 5S because each of the actions is a word that begins with "S".

- Sort.
- Set in Order.
- Shine.
- Standardize.
- Sustain.

Each of these is defined on the following pages.

5S - Sort

Sort means to identify potentially unneeded items, evaluate their usefulness, and deal with them appropriately.
- Use the red tag process to identify potentially unneeded items.
- Each of the red tagged items is evaluated for usefulness.
- Each item is dealt with appropriately.

Sort Comes First. Remember, sort comes first because you don't want to find a place for, organize, or clean something that shouldn't even be there. Sort helps eliminate the "pack rat" mentality.

Red Tag Questions. As you identify potentially unneeded items, ask yourself these three questions:
1. Do we need this item?
2. If we need it, do we need this many of them?
3. If we need it, does it need to be located here?

Note: If in doubt, red tag it. Be careful of people who tell you that if you are in doubt, you must throw it out. This can get you in deep trouble. I've seen people throw away valuable or much needed items simply because they hadn't been used in a while. That's crazy. And there is one thing that Lean is not – it's not crazy.

A couple of years ago I had an initial meeting with a metal stamper. In this meeting were the Executive Team and several middle managers. As we were discussing Lean and I was sharing my methods with them, I mentioned the tool 5S.

Immediately, the VP of Operations said, *"Don't use the word 5S around here! You may get attacked!"* I was like, *"What? Why, what's going on?"* *"Well,"* he explained, *"we had a Lean consultant come in to help us last year. She told us that if something hasn't moved in three weeks, dump it!"* I looked at him and said, *"You didn't!"* He said, *"Oh, yes we did!"* Without thinking, I blurted out, *"Are you completely out of your minds?"*

I got hired! Think about it. They had probably 1000 jobs that they'd run at some point. All of those jobs have tools, fixtures, gages…you get the picture right? And how many of those jobs have run in the last three weeks? Not many, I'm guessing! So you're going to throw everything out? That's beyond dumb! That's stupid! And there is one thing that Lean is not, and that's stupid. You must use your head! Start with some of those jobs that haven't run since 1962! There's plenty to eliminate if you use your head and basic facts. This company was almost brought to its knees because of poor advice.

5S - Set in Order

Set in Order means that you organize things so that they are easy to use and identify them so that anyone can find them and put them away within 30 seconds.
- Organize things so anyone can find and/or put them back quickly.
- Every Lean technique fits within the definition of Set in Order because they revolve around eliminating waste by organizing things.
- Create visual systems so that what needs to be done is visual and obvious to everyone.

Organize and locate items based on how often you use them:
- Level 1: If you use it constantly... store it within arm's reach.
- Level 2: If you use it frequently... store it close by.
- Level 3: If you use it infrequently... store it out of the way.
- Level 4: If it is under evaluation... store it out back (red tag it).

5S - Shine

Shine is the process of keeping your area neat, clean, spotless, shiny, and white.
- Keep your area clean, spotless, shiny, and white.
- The goal is to "be clean", not "to clean".
- Use the strategies of "contain" and "prevent" to reduce the need to clean while improving shine – never let it get dirty and you won't have to clean.
- White is used because it shows dirt.

The goal is to "be clean", not "to clean". Many people equate 5S with cleaning. 5S is then reduced to just cleaning things, and since most people hate cleaning, they'll run in the opposite direction when 5S is mentioned.

It's important to remember that Shine means to "be clean". Our theoretically perfect goal is to "be clean" without having "to clean".

Two concepts are critical: contain and prevent. How do you reach a goal of "clean" without having to clean? The answer is to contain and prevent. Contain dirt, dust, fluids, and other messes. Prevent them from ever getting things dirty.

We frustrate people tremendously when we fixate on clean, clean, clean when there is no hope of it staying that way. I've seen machines that create such messes that cleaning would be a 24/7 job and still not be up to standard. This has a way of demoralizing people. First, fix the leaks, capture the scrap, redesign and rebuild the hydraulic system so hoses don't burst, then set your Shine goal with some reasonable expectation of reaching it.

So we don't have to clean? Can you contain and prevent everything? No. You will still have to clean. But your focus should be on containing and preventing so that you can reduce the time it takes to clean. Clean a little bit all the time and you will prevent having to spend tons of time later.

Cleaning is actually waste. Did you know that the act of cleaning is actually waste? It doesn't add value. I know, we must be clean and spotless, but that doesn't necessarily mean we need to increase our cleaning time. Spend more time containing and preventing so that your cleaning time goes down and your bright shiny goes up.

Most people hate to clean. When we have idle time we ask people to clean – something they hate to do. This is counterproductive because people will do anything in their power to avoid it. They spend all their energy getting out of it, so cleaning doesn't get done anyway. Focus their energy on containing and preventing the mess so they don't have to clean. The better they do at it, the less they have to clean – that's a great incentive! As they accomplish this, I'll bet they improve other things along the way as well.

Shine is not a goal – it's a measurement. This is going to sound weird, but I look at how people have achieved Shine as a measure of how well they own the objective of "improvement". It measures the degree to which they're stepping up to get things done or how well they "get it"!

The place I go to see how people are stepping up, or how well they've embraced the process, is the men's bathroom on the production floor. One glance tells me where people are at.

5S - Standardize

The purpose of Standardize is that once you have "perfected" a process, make it a standard that everyone follows.

- Standardize all of your work actions and procedures.
- Standardizing supports effective implementation of sort, set in order, and shine.
- Once you've perfected a process, make it a standard that everyone follows.

Without standardize, the following will probably happen:

- Over a period of time, things go back to the way they were.
- Stuff accumulates as work is done.
- Desks, tables, and equipment begin to accumulate clutter.
- Contain and prevent falls away and messes accumulate.

Every person must know exactly what their responsibilities are. What must be done, how to do it, when to do it, and where it must be done must be clear and visual to each person.

5S - Sustain

Sustain means that we do what we say we're going to do. It involves making a habit of performing in the correct way. Perfected processes and systems are the quickest way to achieve Sustain.
- Make a habit of maintaining standardized procedures.
- Follow through is important.
- Sustainability is critical to success.

If Sustain is not accomplished, the following will occur:
- As soon as you Sort, things begin to accumulate again.
- As soon as you Set in Order, things don't get put back.
- As soon as something is cleaned, it gets dirty again.

Sustain is the most difficult of the 5S's.
- Sustain is difficult if your processes are not as good as they could or should be.
- With a perfect process, Sustain is easy.
- With a bad process, Sustain is nearly impossible.
- If things begin to deteriorate, it's a sure sign that you need to improve your process.

If you think it's a people issue...
- It probably is not. It's more than likely a process problem.
- Improve the process and everyone becomes brilliant.

Do you want to "sustain" easily?
- Create a perfect process.
- Earn everyone's trust and respect.

No one will want to mess it up!

Kaizen

Kaizen has become a word we use to describe a focused, high energy, three to five day process where we blitz an area that needs improvement. A small group of people can make major improvements in a short period of time using this method. These Kaizen events can be 5S, setup improvement, layout, administrative, or other event.

In reality, Kaizen means "continuous improvement". It is a process where everyone gets involved in the improvement process while spending very little money. If you think about it, you've been doing this in a variety of ways since the day you were born. It's just that now you need to be more intentional about it. Every person must improve what they're doing every day. Improvements with Kaizen are typically small and incremental. However, that doesn't mean the results are small. Remember, small things become big things when repeated over a period of time. Too many times people will discount continuous improvement in favor of innovation. Innovation is flashy and glamorous. It solves a problem in a new way. But to be truly successful we need both continuous improvement and innovation. Innovation is typically implemented by a small group of managers and key support people. It is many times out of the reach of a normal hourly person. So if an organization is "innovation driven", it leaves most people out of the loop. In this "innovation" process people become detached, uncooperative, and negative. But continuous improvement gets everyone involved, cooperating, and focused on the positive. That is the reason why it is so powerful.

Kaizen Event: Benefits and Drawbacks

Benefits:
- An area that is critical to your success can be selected.
- Improvements are made in a short period of time – typically three to five days.
- Generates enthusiasm and energy.
- Focus is on one specific area or process, not everything at once.
- Reduces bureaucracy and barriers within the team.
- Focuses resources.
- They have a great payback.
- Creates a foundation of improvement.

Drawbacks:
- Key resources are tied up for the event period.
- Decisions are made on the fly, sometimes with not enough research or input.
- Too many events can suck resources dry and leave too many homework assignments that probably won't get done.

- Can be inefficient – within the event there can be a lot of standing around, waiting for things.

Value Stream Mapping

Value Stream Mapping is a process that links all of the Lean activities in one value stream through systematic data gathering and analysis. A value stream is every step, value added or not, that an organization takes to turn raw material into a finished product. There are numerous value streams in any organization. They can encompass office or manufacturing, or in many cases, both. So it is a tool that can be used by anyone. This tool "maps" the flow of all information and materials through the system.

A Value Stream Map identifies, gathers data, analyzes, and makes improvements to all the specific activities or steps that occur within the value stream for a specific process, product, or product family. This process reduces waste, improves flow, improves communication, and links all of the people and processes together from supplier to customer to create a sustainable Lean organization.

Value Stream Mapping is fairly straight forward once you get used to it. But it takes a while to get there. Your best bet is to train someone internally to lead this process. If you initiate Value Stream Mapping without any foundational work, you're asking for trouble. Every Value Stream Mapping book I've read will admit that people must have a desire to do it before you should attempt it. But they offer little information on how to get people to that point. It is best to incorporate this tool once you get everyone moving in a positive direction and they are ready to take it on.

SMED – Single Minute Exchange of Dies

SMED is an acronym for "Single Minute Exchange of Dies". The goal is to complete a setup in single digits of time, or in nine minutes or less. Some people mistakenly think the name implies that the setup or changeover should take one minute or less, but that's not true.

Setup Time Reduction – What's it Worth?

Some people immediately recognize the value of improving setup time. Others simply say, *"What's the big deal! It doesn't take that long! We've got bigger issues than that to fix!"*

For me, the major thought process is this: "small things become big things when repeated over a period of time". So maybe you only save 10 minutes on each setup. But how many setups do you do over a period of time?

Quicker setups will:
1. Create capacity.
    - 20 minutes saved per setup, at 10 setups per week will gain you over 4 weeks of actual machine time over a period of one year.
    - Improve total run time or efficiency.
        - With every detail being managed, the

machine will run better (fewer shutdowns) and more efficiently (faster). This allows the machine to run the job quicker, leading to more capacity.
- 10 percent saved on run time will create over five weeks of machine time over a period of one year.
- Combined, that equals nearly 10 weeks of open time on the machine per year – remember this is one shift only.

2. Simplify your process.
- When you create quicker setups you eliminate waste and extra steps. The job gets easier. There is less to remember. This means there is less to forget and stress out about.

3. Decrease "work in process" inventory.
- When you can set up quickly, you can reduce your lot size because you are more flexible. You can setup on the fly so you need less inventory "just in case". Smaller lot sizes means less inventory, less space to store it, less borrowed money or interest expense, and less confusion.
- If you reduce your setup time by 50 percent you can effectively double the amount of setups without increasing the total time

spent on setups.

4. Decrease lead time and improve response time to the customer.
   - With a shorter setup time you are more flexible – you can setup the job more times if needed. This means when a customer calls up, we can get parts to them quickly. We call this decreased lead time, or better yet, better "response" time to the customer. When we run large lots because our setup time is long, we need to wait for the run to get done in order to respond to the customer – this causes delays.

5. Improve quality.
   - Setup improvements demand that you manage every detail of the process. The more details you manage, or improve, the better your quality. Scrap rates tend to go down with improvement in setup time.

6. Decrease tooling costs.
   - When you manage all the details you are in reality "perfecting the tools". Perfected tools and processes lead to less wear and breakage. Less wear and breakage means lower tooling costs.

7. Decrease "looking" time.
    - Managing all the details includes organizing every element of the job and tooling. As you organize, less time is spent looking for things.

The list could go on. You can see that reduced setup time affects many other critical areas. Reducing setup time is one of the highest priorities when you have a desire to be more competitive. It's a major component of being the "best in the world".

Total Productive Maintenance (TPM)

Definition

TPM is a method of improving and maximizing equipment uptime and efficiencies through the systematic application of several levels of equipment maintenance and design carried out by, and involving, every person in the organization.

Goals

The goals of TPM include:
1. To improve the effectiveness of each person.
2. To create and sustain a sense of ownership within each person.
3. To improve and maximize equipment uptime.
4. To improve and maximize equipment efficiency.
5. To reduce operational costs.
6. To reduce throughput time.
7. To improve customer response time.
8. To achieve zero breakdowns.
9. To achieve zero defects.

Critical Factors

The following inputs help to better understand the definition and goals of TPM:

1. **Everyone is involved**. Every person in the organization must be involved, from front to back. Every person has responsibilities within TPM, from design and/or planning, to daily application requirements. The tendency is to mistakenly think that only the maintenance department should get involved. In reality, every person must take personal responsibility for the TPM requirements in their area, on their machine, or within their authority.

2. **Think ownership, not compliance**. Compliance is easier to get than ownership, but it implies compliance to a "*minimum*" standard. You don't want minimum, you want "*best in the world*". That is achieved only through ownership of the goal.

3. **Think "*perfect*", not "*good enough*"**. Our theoretically perfect goal is zero breakdowns and 100 percent OEE (Overall Equipment Effectiveness). This is only accomplished through the single-minded pursuit of perfection.

4. **Maintenance people must change their mindset**. Maintenance people often tell me their job is to fix things when they break. If that mindset isn't changed, nothing improves. We simply react to breakdowns, which means we are held hostage by them. Maintenance people should be like firefighters – they should spend the bulk of their time preventing breakdowns and a small portion of their time putting out fires, or fixing things. Remember, all of us are maintenance people for our own area or processes!

5. **Anticipate what can happen**. When do things break down? Yes, things break down when you least expect it and at the worst possible time. Your job is to anticipate what can go wrong. Kind of like an FMEA (Failure Modes and Effect analysis) for the entire process.

6. **Be like the Maytag repairman**. What makes the Maytag repairman lonely? The machines don't break down! Why is that? Because everyone in the system, from design, to manufacturing, to shipping, is focused on the goal of reliability. This is a great example of TPM.

7. **Coordinate all departments**. Every department must identify and take ownership of their TPM responsibilities, including designing, maintaining, and using the equipment.

8. **Measure and document all downtime**. Machines go down for lots of reasons. Every one of them must be documented and charted. Then attack each one systematically.

Responsibilities within TPM

Every person and every department must embrace their responsibility within TPM. Some of those responsibilities include:
- Operator – inspect, clean, lubricate, adjust, collect data, observe, and measure.
- Maintenance – all of the duties of an operator, and repair, replace, schedule, rebuild, determine spare parts quantities, and requirements, order and organize spare parts, design for zero breakdowns, design for maximum speeds and feeds, design for containment of oils, coolants, and offal.
- Engineering – design for zero breakdowns, design for maximum speeds and feeds, design for simple and quick replacement, design for use of off-the-shelf components, develop data collection sheets, develop scoreboards and

measurement systems, design for work and process flow, design for containment of oils, coolants, and offal.
- Management – set goals for zero breakdowns, set goals for speeds and feeds, develop data collection sheets, develop scoreboards and measurement systems, include progress to goals in weekly and monthly progress meeting agendas, assist in creating action plans and strategies.

Kanban

What is Kanban?

- Kanban is the communication system for Lean Manufacturing.
- The purpose of Kanban is to reduce "overproduction' which is one of the worst "eight deadly wastes".
- The goal of Kanban is to produce only what is needed, when it is needed, in the quantities needed by the customer.
- The word Kanban in Japanese means "card" or "sign" and identifies the card used in a Pull System.
- A Kanban System is an information system that fully integrates your entire process, connecting customer demand to each of your processes. It communicates the "pull" from the customer back up through each process.
- A Pull System is a system where each process pulls product from the upstream process. Each process only produces enough products to replace what was pulled. The trigger, or initial pull, is a customer order.
- Rather than produce to an estimate of sales, or base production on past experience, a Pull System produces to demand.

The Goals of Kanban

The "theoretically perfect" goal for Kanban is:
- Zero "work in process" inventory.
- Zero overproduction.
- Zero waste.
- Integration of your entire process, starting with the customer, and back up through your processes all the way to your supplier.

To reach this goal, you begin with enough Kanbans in the system to support the current situation, and gradually reduce the number of Kanbans by either of the following methods:
- Reduce the number of Kanbans until you discover problems, and then fix the problems.
- Improve the process or eliminate problems so that the number of Kanbans can be reduced.

Action Plans to Create a Kanban System

- Eliminate waste so as to improve cycle time, reduce number of people required, reduce floor space required, and improve flow.
- Work toward one piece flow to eliminate "work in process" inventory, space between operations, and excess movement of people or materials.
- Pull product through the system – the customer begins the pull process.

- Any process produces only the quantity that was pulled from them.
- Any part pulled from a process must be free of defects.
- The Kanban or card, follows the parts.
- Production at each stage must be leveled for even flow.
- With improvements, the number of Kanbans can be reduced.

Pareto Analysis

Pareto Analysis was created by an Italian mathematician and economist by the name of "Vilfredo Pareto".

He lived from 1848 to 1923 and was known for his law called, "The Law of Disproportionate Distribution". He based his "law" on economic data that he collected. This "data" showed him an interesting set of facts. He found that 80 percent of Italy's wealth was controlled by 20 percent of the population.

For many of us, this doesn't seem very noteworthy, but what Vilfredo had discovered was what we call the 80/20 rule. This rule is in evidence around us every day, whether we realize it or not. For example, when we have a list of things to do, we naturally sort or prioritize that list into what's most important to do first. That's Pareto's principle in action.

Today, we use Pareto Analysis to intentionally help us focus our attention. Consider how Pareto's work has been, or can be used or applied, to various everyday situations:

- 80 percent of sales come from 20 percent of your customers.
- 80 percent of scrap comes from 20 percent of the causes of scrap.

Got Lean? Law #6

- 80 percent of breakdowns come from 20 percent of the causes of breakdowns.
- 80 percent of a process improvement comes from 20 percent of your effort.
- 80 percent of your success comes from 20 percent of what you do.
- 80 percent of your attendance problems come from 20 percent of your people.
- 80 percent of your accidents come from 20 percent of the causes.

How much of an advantage, and how important is it to your success, to *"know"* the facts behind the 20 percent in each of the above situations? It really helps you focus your attention and quite possibly increases your effectiveness a hundred fold.

Does this mean that Pareto Analysis or the 80/20 rule can predict every result in your organization? No, but it does get us thinking about what we spend time on. Why spend time on the "trivial many" problems that come up? We must instead focus on the "important few" if we are going to be successful. In each case, we must look at our "input" or "effort", and our "results" or "output". There is not always a one to one relationship between the two. You must focus on "results", not "activities".

So, what does Pareto Analysis do for us? Well, it helps us understand that there are many reasons or causes for what is happening and it disciplines us to focus on those causes that are most important. This saves valuable time as you fix things quickly and effectively, leading to improvements in many areas, such as:

- Capacity.
- Safety.
- On-time delivery.
- Attendance.
- Scrap.
- Downtime.
- Customer complaints.
- Material shortages.
- All types of errors.
- Inventory discrepancies.

Each of these areas is critical to your success.

Got Lean? Law #6

Study the information below. Given the Pareto chart shown, what would you work on first?

1. Data collection sheet:

Code #	May	June	July	Total
1																15
2	||||	||||-||	||||-||	19
3	||||-|||	|||| ||||	|||| |||| ||||-|	34
4	||·	||	|||	7
5														11
6	||||	||||	||||-|||	17

2. Trend Chart:

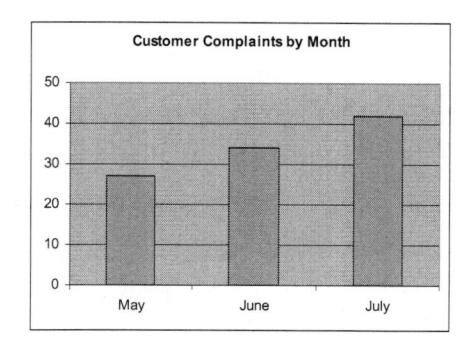

Customer Complaints by Month

Codes:
#1 = Other
#2 = Shipping error
#3 = Quality Problem
#4 = Pricing
#5 = Invoice error
#6 = Late delivery

3. Pareto Chart:

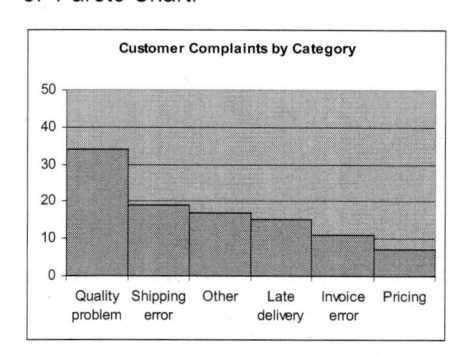

Customer Complaints by Category
(Quality problem, Shipping error, Other, Late delivery, Invoice error, Pricing)

5W's and an H

Your ability to ask questions and gather facts is the most important tool you can pull out of your toolbox – bar none. It can be wielded instantly, it can calm people down, it can dig for facts, it can get people thinking, it can create instant energy, and it can instantly challenge someone to step up. No other tool can claim such power and versatility.

The use of this tool includes asking the questions, who, what, when, where, why, and how. They do not have to be asked in any order. You do not try to solve the problem, give causes, point blame or guess. You simply ask questions. The best way to practice asking questions is to create a worksheet like that found on the next page. Make 20 copies and number them 1 to 20. Each week, pick a problem, issue, or situation. Write a one sentence description at the top of the page. Then brainstorm all the possible questions you can think of on the subject, placing them in the correct category. After brainstorming, select the three questions that you think will get you the biggest return on your invested time. Answer them by collecting facts to get to the next level of questions.

This tool of asking questions takes practice. It is a learned skill. If you practice this once a week for 20 weeks, you'll start to get the hang of it.

Got Lean?   Law #6

5W's and an H
Worksheet

Description:

Who:

What:

When:

Where:

Why:

How:

Miscellaneous:

Got Lean? Law #6

5W's and an H Worksheet Example

Description: Late pizza deliveries on weekends (30 minutes or free)

Who: Who is responsible?
Who are the drivers?
Who delivers most of the late pizzas?

What: What directions are given?
What are the obstacles?
What time creates most late pizzas?
What is the number one reason for late deliveries?
What are the obstacles to delivering on time?

When: When in the 30 minutes are drivers given the pizza?
When are people ordering the most pizzas?

Where: Where are late pizzas being delivered?
Where is the waste in the process?
Where is our delivery area?

Why: Why do we have this 30 minute or free policy?
Why are pizzas late?

How: How much time is it taking to make pizza?
How much time is driver given?
How long from order taken to kitchen?

Miscellaneous: Are all areas of delivery area affected?
Is problem in the kitchen or with the drivers?

Initial Focus:
1) What is this costing us? You don't want to spend time on a low priority issue.
2) What is the number one reason for late deliveries? You'll have to gather some data, but the data should pinpoint the specific cause!

Conclusion

The tools of Lean assist us in reaching our goal of finding and eliminating waste to become more competitive. It is important to remember that a tool is just a tool. Using a tool is not the goal. It is an action taken to reach the goal. Start with simple tools and work toward the more complex. Also, use a tool appropriate to the situation you're in.

Critical concepts learned in this chapter involve some of the basic tools of Lean:
- 5S.
- Kaizen.
- Value Stream Mapping.
- SMED (Singe Minute Exchange of Dies).
- TPM (Total Productive Maintenance).
- Kanban.
- Pareto Analysis.
- 5W's and an H.

Practice Exercise: Law #6

Complete the following and check your answers with the answer sheet found on page 222. Do not treat this as a test. The goal is not to get a high grade, but to get them all correct. If you don't know an answer, look back through the materials to find it.

1. The goal of Lean is:
    a. To use a tool.
    b. To find and eliminate waste.
    c. To use Value Stream Mapping.
    d. To pick the low hanging fruit.
    e. To get rid of as many people as possible.

2. Kaizen means _____ improvement and focuses on one specific area of _____ in a _____ period of time.

3. What is the goal of a maintenance person?
    a. Fix what breaks. Are you kidding?
    b. Smoke cigarettes, drink coffee, and talk about hunting.
    c. Zero breakdowns.
    d. Preventative maintenance.
    e. Keep a list.

4. The old tools we used are no longer useful.
    a. True.
    b. False.

Got Lean? Law #6

5. Reducing setup time is a high priority if we want to:
    a. Keep everyone busy.
    b. Be the best in the world.
    c. Reduce costs.
    d. Upset the grizzled veterans.
    e. B and C.
    f. None of the above.

6. If you hate to clean:
    a. Avoid it when possible.
    b. Hire people to do it for you.
    c. Contain and prevent the mess.
    d. Volunteer for something you're good at.

7. Faster setups will improve _____ time to our customers.

8. 5S is a tool that focuses on cleaning:
    a. True.
    b. False.

9. We fail in the use of the tools because we like to throw tools at people who:
    a. Don't "get it".
    b. "Get it".
    c. Are busy.
    d. Can't catch.
    e. Can catch, but can't see.

Got Lean? Law #6

10. Pareto Analysis was created by:
    a. Pareto Heimlich.
    b. Vilfredo Pareto.
    c. Some dude in Italy.
    d. Joe Scanlon in the 1920's.
    e. Someone at Toyota.

11. If you are going to "shine" effectively, what must you do?
    a. Try to get someone else to do it.
    b. Contain and prevent the mess in the first place.
    c. Spend more time at it than you are now.
    d. Hire someone to do it.

12. The most important tool in your toolbox is:
    a. A bigger hammer.
    b. Five W's and an H.
    c. Value Stream Mapping.
    d. 5S.
    e. Kanban.

13. If your process deteriorates over a period of time:
    a. People should be written up.
    b. Blame another department.
    c. Complain to management.
    d. Your process is not as good as it could or should be.

Got Lean? Law #6

14. Which of the following is **not** true of Pareto Analysis:
    a. It utilizes facts, not opinions.
    b. It focuses on solutions.
    c. It focuses on those causes that will have the greatest impact.
    d. It reduces or eliminates discussions and arguments.

15. Tools should be used:
    a. That fit the situation.
    b. That prove how smart you are.
    c. That creates the most detail in the shortest period of time.
    d. From simple to most difficult over time.
    e. Both A and D.

16. Anyone can find anything, or put it back, within _____.

17. If "sustain" is achieved:
    a. Be thankful you got assigned to a good team.
    b. It's because you have more than one 20 percenter on your team.
    c. Things will still begin deteriorating.
    d. It means you've successfully implemented and maintained the first four S's.

Got Lean? Law #6

18. If in doubt:
    a. Throw it out.
    b. Your supervisor should decide.
    c. Red tag it.
    d. Give it away.
    e. Store it appropriately.

19. The goal of "shine" is:
    a. "Be clean".
    b. "To clean".
    c. Harass the help by making them clean more.
    d. Foolish, because it just gets dirty again.
    e. Hire it done.

20. If you use it constantly, it should be stored:
    a. Within arms reach.
    b. Close by.
    c. Out of the way.
    d. Out back.
    e. Overhead.

Got Lean?

Law #6: Lean is a Set of Tools, or Methods, for Finding and Eliminating Waste

Self Assessment

No				Yes		
1	2	3	4	5	1)	Have we eliminated the "one tool" fixation?
1	2	3	4	5	2)	Did we start with simple tools?
1	2	3	4	5	3)	Are we still using the old tools when appropriate?
1	2	3	4	5	4)	Have we eliminated the expectation that people use tools before they "get it"?
1	2	3	4	5	5)	Do we use 5S to initiate action and get people involved?
1	2	3	4	5	6)	Does 5S mean something besides "cleaning" to our people?
1	2	3	4	5	7)	Are Kaizen events used appropriately?
1	2	3	4	5	8)	Is Value Stream Mapping helping us find and eliminate waste?
1	2	3	4	5	9)	Has SMED reduced setup time?
1	2	3	4	5	10)	Has TPM reduced breakdowns?
1	2	3	4	5	11)	Is Kanban effectively reducing overproduction and integrating our process?
1	2	3	4	5	12)	Are we using Pareto Analysis to identify priorities?
1	2	3	4	5	13)	Are we effectively using 5 W's and an H?

Law #6: Lean is a Set of Tools, or Methods, for Finding and Eliminating Waste

Group Discussion Questions

1. Given the self assessment questions on the previous page, what are your organization's:

    a. Strengths:

    b. Weaknesses:

2. Why is it important to make sure people "get it" before introducing a more complex tool?

3. Why is it dangerous to allow 5S to merely become a code word for cleaning?

4. Why is it important to include people when using any tool on a process that involves them?

5. Describe what is meant by, "use tools appropriate to the situation"?

Got Lean? Law #6

Practice Exercise Answer Sheet

1. B
2. Continuous, process, short
3. C
4. B
5. E
6. C
7. Response
8. B
9. A
10. B
11. B
12. B
13. D
14. B
15. E
16. 30 seconds
17. D
18. C
19. A
20. A

Leadership for Sustainability

Leadership for Sustainability

Given everything we've discussed so far you might think that formal leadership can coast. After all, everyone is pitching in, right? Well, nothing could be farther from the truth! Leading this process will consume all of your energy and attention. It is not only Lean Sustainability at stake here...it is the future of your organization! It's the whole enchilada! So you better get this right!

As you know, leadership is a huge issue. We can't begin to cover it all here, but I will address those areas that are critical to your success. The thoughts I share here will both identify areas where many organizations get it wrong and also thoughts on how you can lead more effectively.

Ignoring or underestimating a negative culture. A negative culture can contribute to diminished output – many people admit that they could improve output by as much as 80 percent just by changing the negative culture to a positive culture. Yet, many leaders either ignore or underestimate the power of this culture! Worse yet, some leaders won't even admit that their culture is not where it should be! I don't know if they think that admitting it shows weakness, if it's just frustration on their part, or if it's simply pride. Maybe it's lack of knowledge on how to change it, or simply ignorance about how powerful culture can be. Maybe they're just impatient to get results. I'm sure there are several reasons. But I know this – many leaders don't see the need to address the culture. They want to just jump into the tools. What typically sells them on addressing the culture is the fact that they've tried their previous methods several times and they either haven't worked, or have failed completely. As a leader, you must build your foundation. There are no shortcuts. If you get it wrong, you have to start over. And it gets tougher to do each time, so you might as well do it correctly, right from the start.

I remember a situation in which the new president of an organization was trying to make changes. He came from a well established company with a great culture. He had absolutely no skills in changing the negative culture he found himself in! He was totally overwhelmed! He looked at the skilled workers and thought that they could accomplish great things. And he was right. Except that these people were 30 year grizzled veterans with no intention of changing. He had no clue what to do. He didn't even know what it was or how to describe it to me! When I described what was going on and the process required to change it, he was not happy. Like it, or not, though, he didn't really have a choice. There are no shortcuts. Better to roll up your sleeves and get to work!

What's most disturbing to me is the trend of outsourcing work to other countries because of the inability to compete. I understand the need to compete, but I wonder about how much time and effort has been put into improving locally first. Actually, that's not right. Much time and effort has been spent. Many organizations have spent years and have tried many methods with limited results. But, I question the method and tactics and the way they've been applied. I know of several organizations that are pulling work back in because they have found a way to tap into the 20- 80 percent improvement that can be found through the conversion from negative to positive energy. The question is: *"How committed are you to tapping into this huge reservoir of competitive advantage?"*

I don't mean to sound arrogant or condescending, but most leaders give up too soon or underestimate what it takes. Don't you be one of those!

It's all about respect. Being an effective leader is all, and completely about, respect for every person. Empowerment begins and ends with respect. If you do not respect people...every person... you will struggle with anything beyond compliance. This respect can't be faked – people will see right through you. Everything you say, everything you do, every non-verbal, every decision, every question, every contact you have with other people speaks to your respect, or lack of respect, for them. Respect must be genuine and freely given. The foundation of any successful company is respect for people.

Trust is earned. Do you want to tear apart your organization? Just do something to tear down trust...like say one thing and do another. It will destroy your organization from the inside. Everything you say and do either earns trust or tears it down. Leadership must constantly examine themselves in the area of trust. Remember, all it takes is one person in a leadership position to destroy trust.

I remember an organization I was working with that was struggling. They "won" a hard-fought seven dollar an hour pay concession from their hourly people. These same people also gave up their holiday and vacation pay! Guess what happened when they found out that the support staff received a three percent raise at the same time?

Model the behavior. If you want people to behave professionally and with integrity, then you need to model the behavior. Any department or organization will take on the traits of the person leading it. So if you want to see your impact, look at how people in your department or organization act. You must lead them to respect people, earn trust, build relationships, work with integrity, hustle, get meaningful things done quickly, and work toward perfection and excellence in everything they do. You must set the tone, you must model the behavior! You must challenge them. You must teach them to be self managed so that they in turn can model the behavior. Your future depends on it!

Work with integrity. Integrity is saying what you're going to do, and doing what you say, when you said you were going to do it. It's about respecting people and earning their trust. Work with honor, be honest, gather facts, and don't blow smoke at people.

Lose the ego. There are people in leadership that have huge egos. They aren't about to respect people or earn their trust because they feel it's beneath them. They think they're better than everyone else. This attitude must be purged from your organization because it kills productivity!

A leader's job is to empower. Empowering people means to create an environment in which people want to, and do, take ownership for results. A leader's job is to create the environment. Here are several ways to accomplish that:

1. **Respect others**. Begin practicing behaviors that show respect. If you are not practicing these

behaviors now, or struggle with them, you must not do anything else until you are using them with some success. If you practice the behaviors consistently, you'll find that your own attitude will change – do not wait for your attitude to change before you take positive action. Here are the behaviors that show me that someone respects me:

- They look me in the eye.
- They include me in discussions that affect me or my job.
- They look out for me and my interests.
- They are gracious.
- They disagree with me when necessary, but are not disagreeable when they do.
- They keep their mouths shut when appropriate.
- They treat me like they would a customer or the president of the company, even if I'm not.
- They set clear expectations and boundaries.
- They are upfront and honest, they share information freely.
- They listen without passing judgment.
- They don't dictate, they ask questions to better understand me and develop my skills.

- They respect me even during the times I don't deserve it.
- They're patient.
- They know what's important and what's not – they don't major on the minors.
- They take the time to find out who I am and how I tick.
- If something is wrong with my work or job, they discuss it immediately with me first, not after rumors start and they're forced to.
- They value my contribution.
- They are open to influence. They let me improve on the final product/process.

2. **Involve others**. Find ways to get people involved in their job. Expect them to solve their own problems. Give them information. Ask questions when they have a problem – don't just solve the problem for them. Open up problems for discussion or start a small team to correct a nagging problem. However, do not try to do everything for everybody!

3. **Don't announce – just do it!** Rather than announcing that major changes are taking place and everything will be different, just start doing what you need to do. Starting with high expectations only sets you up for failure

because you won't possibly be able to do everything anyway. And if you don't get everything done it just gives the 30 percenters fuel. Which reminds me, this isn't about you, it's about them. Don't announce – Just do it!

4. **Don't set yourself up for failure**. Many tries at empowerment begin with management telling people "we want to get you involved – we want your ideas – give them to us and we'll use them." This is doomed for failure because if you have 10 people who contribute 10 ideas, that's 100 ideas. The supervisor tries hard and accomplishes 10 of the 100 ideas only to have people say, *"I gave them all kinds of ideas and they haven't done one of mine yet."* People will either think their supervisor is incompetent or that he/she wasn't interested in their ideas in the first place! Most times, neither is true! What you want is for people to solve their own problems, not have someone else be responsible for them. Start slowly and build consistently and steadily. Many companies try to do everything at once and the whole process ends up dying in a ball of flames. Remember, every time you have to start this process over again, multiply by a difficulty factor of 100. It's not important how many ideas a person generates – it's how many they implement.

5. **Set clear expectations**. Get people involved in setting goals for themselves and establishing visual measurements. Help them set simple job related, quality, and delivery goals and teach them how to graph them. Remember, this may be new to them – lead them, don't mandate. Challenge them but be careful you don't overdo this in the early days. Also give them clear boundaries. If you ask them to solve a problem, don't set the boundaries after they come back with a recommendation – do it before.

6. **Critique their thought process, not the decision**. They may make mistakes early on. If they do, walk them through their thought process to help develop their skills and analyze the options at the point they went wrong. Don't just criticize their decision. Help them grow from the experience.

7. **Assist in building skills**. Discover what skills they need and get them training to fill the gaps. This includes technical, interpersonal, problem solving skills, etc. Creating the environment means building the competence level of every person.

8. **Feed the 20 percenters**. In a typical situation, 20 percent of the people willingly embrace the

changes and you can depend on them to help drive the program. Another 50 percent are fence-sitters. They're not hostile but they're not helping like they should either. The remaining 30 percent are resisters. They are antagonistic toward change and often deliberately try to make it fail. The resisters are often the most vocal and love it when you give them lots of attention. Your focus must be on feeding the 20 percent. The 20 percent must identify the 50 percent and win them over. Don't let anyone allow the 30 percent to drag them into the pit. Focus on the 20 percent and the 50 percent – you're 70 percent of the way if you accomplish that much. Many of the remaining 30 percent will convert when they see the results, or lose their power.

9. **Latch on to a mentor and don't let go**. One of the things you need to do is establish contact with people who are good at respecting and empowering others. A good way to improve your own skills as a leader is to observe, emulate, and ask lots of questions of these people. A good relationship with a mentor will help you pick up skills more quickly than doing it on your own.

10. **Remember who your customer is**. You're job as a team leader, supervisor, or manager is to

unleash the creativity, energy, and skills of those around you. In other words, the people that report to you are your "customers" and you provide a service to them. Concentrate on providing excellent service by creating an environment in which they can be successful. How happy are your customers with the environment you've created for them? Is it an environment in which they can be successful? If they had a choice, would they willingly choose you as their boss? Fact: the number one reason people quit their job is because of their direct supervisor!

11. **Help them solve their own problems**. Don't get caught in the trap of simply giving the answer to a problem, even if you know the answer. Instead, ask questions that assist each person to solve the problem themselves. Remember, it's not your problem, it's theirs. They must solve it, not you. Your job is to assist and consult. If your team cannot solve problems on their own, look first at yourself. Do you expect them to solve it themselves? Or do you give them the easy answer, tying them to you permanently, and virtually guaranteeing they won't step up next time!

12. **Learn to Listen.** Your best tool as a leader is to listen. You do this by asking appropriate questions. This is not as easy as it sounds. Effective listening is a very difficult skill to master because we know too much, we're judgmental, we're too busy, we're the boss...right? Effective leaders are great listeners...they ask great questions. Need practice? Go back to the tools section and read the page on 5W's and an H. Do what it says for practice.

Redefine accountability. Most people think of accountability as taking punitive action when people don't do as their told. But if you do this, you'll get compliance as a result. Believe me, you'll never get to be the best if all people do is comply. You must view accountability through the eyes of empowerment. The best way to create accountability is through ownership, and ownership comes through involvement, the setting of clear expectations, and keeping score with scoreboards personal enough for people to step up to take action. When people in your organization complain about the lack of accountability, it's a sure bet that you have not implemented these actions.

Accountability Starts at the Top

I've always said that the closer you get to the top of the organization, the less you can be held accountable by the people within the organization. The closer you get to the top, the more you can do whatever you want with impunity. The sad part is that very few people correct me on this because they agree. Except for people at the top, of course!

Whether you agree or disagree with the above thought, the reality must be this: the higher you go in the organization, the higher the expectations placed on you. As a leader, you cannot shirk this responsibility. But I see many leaders who do shirk it because they can do whatever they want and no one can tell them different!

How do you change this? Create an advisory board of people you respect who will tell you what you need to hear, not what you want to hear. This group should not worry about whether they hurt your feelings. They must also have the necessary savvy, skills, and opportunity to collect facts within the organization so they know what's going on. They need to be your trusted advisory team. Listen to them! Let them hold you accountable!

Grow People who "Get It"

The fastest way to grow people who "get it" is to help them discover and pursue their passion. People who are passionate about something are people who "get it". How do you find out what they're passionate about? Listen to what gets them going. What gets them excited? What are they interested in? What thing draws out their emotion? What are they frustrated with? Along with that, let them choose what to improve. Don't worry if what they start with seems small or inconsequential. They're learning. Let them go.

I was several months into Lean training with a packaging company when the vice president of operations sat me down one day and said, *"I don't know if you realized this, but I was about ready to pull the plug on this training a while back."*

"Why would you have even thought about doing that?" I asked. *"Because"*, he replied, *"I had a group that took on the project of moving a pop machine from the front of the plant to the back of the plant. They spent all this time measuring how many steps they took before and after. They spent huge amounts of time on details. They seemingly wasted all this time on something that to me seemed inconsequential. I thought that if this is all we*

get from this training, we're in a world of hurt! So, I almost pulled the plug!"

"*So why didn't you?*" I asked.

"*Because you told us in training to step back and let our people step up. So I bit my tongue and let it go. Man, am I glad I did. I came real close to doing what we've always done – fail. I realized that I was the one that didn't "get it".*

"*So what happened?*" I asked.

"*It dawned on me that the methods they were using, and the data they were collecting would be the same no matter what the project was. I realized that they were learning the process. And guess what? The second project they took on gained them 43 percent more capacity on their line. Their work was instrumental in getting some new work that we didn't have a clue where to put. I am so glad I didn't pull the plug! What a huge mistake that would have been!*"

When people begin the improvement process they may not choose something that you would choose for them. So be it. Many times, you must let them first improve something that's near and dear to them. If you don't, they'll fixate on it and dig their heels in on your project. They won't do yours anyway. At least not with any speed and enthusiasm. So let them get their pet peeves out of their system. Continue to share information about key performance indicators and what's critically important to our customers and being more competitive – at some point, they'll get to the "good stuff". And don't worry, it will be sooner, rather than later.

People, Process, and Technology

Improvement can come from many different sources. In my experience, though, there are three major sources of these improvements. They include:
- People – people drive improvements. They are the most critical resource you have.
- Process – focus people's attention on improving processes to gain great competitive advantage.
- Technology – there are times when a technology improvement can net you results nothing else can touch.

You must continue to invest in, and upgrade, the above three areas.

The Boss from Hell

I thought about not putting this in the book. It has happened to me, and I've seen it happen to others so many times, I am compelled to include it here.

On several occasions, I have found myself reporting to the boss from hell. The owner, or president, in an effort to inject change and a sense of urgency into the organization, will hire someone to shake up the troops. This person's M.O. is to intimidate, threaten, and belittle people – especially behind closed doors. These people are weak, spineless, egomaniacs, who lead by fear and intimidation. But on the surface and in public they appear to be smooth, polished, and highly effective leaders. They are not!! They are killing your organization! Weed them out! If you need to shake up the troops, follow the laws in this book to inject energy and improve your performance!

It Must Start at the Top?

We've all said this, haven't we? It must start at the top! But does it really? I once had an engineer in a group tell me this in a disgusted tone of voice. The way he said it begged me to ask, *"or what?"* *"Well"*, he said *"if it doesn't start at the top, it's not going to happen!"*

"So if someone at the top doesn't do it, you're all pretty much toast?" I asked. He wasn't sure how to answer that because it didn't seem right. Does it? I mean, that puts you in a situation where there's no hope, right? That's not good! Never put yourself in a position of "no hope". That's crazy! In fact, "it" can start anywhere! I've seen eight dollar an hour hourly people change the

culture of an organization. They lead the process of change! They won't be denied!

As we've said before, change must encompass and involve every person in the organization. I like to have it led by the management team, but it's really, really effective to have everyone learn together. It's great to see a vice president and an hourly person learning together. It makes the VP seem human. It builds relationships...if the manager can swallow their pride, get rid of the ego, and become transparent. Also, if the management team is too far out in front, it may appear as if they are shoving it down everyone's throat!

Consider this from IT services giant Fujitsu, and Steve Perry, head of European Strategy and Operational Development::

> *"While most lean experts say that top management support is critical for an initiative, the approach at Fujitsu has been different. Parry launched his effort and pilot initiatives with backing from his immediate superiors, but without involvement from the very highest levels of the huge Fujitsu hierarchy."*

> *"Six months ago, we were finalists in the U.K. national business awards for customer focus,"* Parry recalls. *"The first thing the CEO knew*

about this was that he had to give a press conference (about the awards)." He said, 'what's this stuff going on?' Then he said, 'that's great, you just carry on doing that.' If we had gone to him in the first place, and talked about subjecting the whole organization to this, he'd have said 'no way.'"

Consistency vs. Flexibility

Most mature organizations are saddled with the negative impact of being too consistent – they have no flexibility! So when they swing in the other direction to full flexibility they create the other negative – no ownership.

These two strategies are opposites when applied to a work situation. If you have complete flexibility, everyone can be shifted to any job at any time. If you have complete consistency, then a person is dedicated to one job and never moves.

Both of these have their benefits and drawbacks.

    Flexibility:
        Benefit – people move to the work to accommodate demand.

> Drawback – no ownership: when everyone is responsible, no one is responsible. It also completely frustrates people because they know the results can improve if they didn't move around all the time.
>
> Consistency:
> Benefit – ownership of results.
> Drawback – limited ability to shift people to accommodate demand.

The goal with these is to do both. Assigning people to a team or cell to create ownership for results, or consistency, is critical to your success. But along with consistency is the need to be flexible enough to shift people for short periods of time. This blend gains you the benefit of both strategies.

Don't Back Off or Ease Up

As a leader, the future of your organization depends on applying the principles I've outlined in this book. Once you begin, don't back off or ease up. You must outlast the negative people who don't think it will work. In fact, people will test you to see if you're serous about it! Is it just another flavor of the month? They'll push you to get you to give up. Don't! Also, don't start something you can't continue because the negative people will use it as fuel. Don't get upset by them, don't disrespect them. Just keep moving forward!

Just because a person says they "get it" doesn't mean they do. The evidence as to whether they get it or not accumulate over a long period of time, not just a day, or week, or month. Anyone can fake it for a while until the heat is off. So, keep the heat on. Observe and measure results, not words or activities. And don't ever back off, ease up, or take your eyes off the prize.

Take the Right People with You

This is perhaps the most difficult question of all: *"Do you have the right people?"* I think it's fair to say that while the goal is to take everyone with you, it's entirely possible not everyone will make it. In fact, the question is, *"how long do I hold on to a person who doesn't get it, and doesn't seem in any mood to get it anytime soon?"* The answer to this question has to do with the situation you're in. If you are in one or more of the following situations, you may have to do something sooner, rather than later:
- Business is tough and there is no time to work with a person who doesn't get it.
- You've worked with the person for some time and they've made little or no progress.
- A person's negative attitude is poisoning others to a point it is no longer tolerable.

- A person is blocking progress and has brought a group to its knees.
- It would be better for the person and the organization if they moved on.

Obviously, this is a tough question, but one that you need to consider seriously. In many cases, you can replace a negative person who disrupts and kills productivity with someone who is positive and gives instant results. It just makes sense to at least consider this with a handful of people who may never get it. They may be killing your culture and your bottom line! In today's economy, you may not have a choice. Remember, though, to do this with respect after some real soul searching.

I know some organizations that still lay off people based on seniority. When you look around, many of the 20 percenters have been laid off and we are surrounded by people who don't want to work, and have no incentive to do so. It demoralizes the 20 percenters who are left. You must change that policy! Layoffs must be based on performance. To do any different is to put your organization at great risk!

Stop Placing Blame and Get Moving

Some people and organizations expend a lot of energy finding and placing blame for actions that took place in the past. This is beyond a complete waste of time, unless you have a time travel machine that allows you to travel back in time to change the action. I'll go out on a limb here and assume that you don't have such a device. So stop it! The only reason to look back is to learn from the mistake. Spend your valuable time and energy improving the culture and the process and moving forward. The motives of anyone continually placing blame should be questioned and put on trial.

Where is Your Focus?

One of the major points I make in Leadership sessions is the need to change the "focus" from the leader to the employee. The focus must not be on the leader – it must be on the person doing the work. Here is another change we must make because the "focus" has traditionally been placed on the leader. The leader has always done everything for everybody! The leader has to control everything. And look at the results of that method – we are surrounded by people who don't "get it" and have a difficult time implementing improvements. As a leader, the focus better not be on you! If it is, you're headed in the wrong direction!

One of the examples of the focus being on the wrong person is when a leader tries to control everything. When a leader is a "controller", the focus is entirely on them. It's good to control things but you can do that without being a "controller". Develop people who are "controllers" of their own job. Keep the focus on them. Then set up methods that help you stay in control, both as a leader and as a team. Scoreboards, project Gantt charts, action plans, and other result focused methods will keep the focus where it belongs – on the people doing the work! I've had leaders come to me after they set this in motion. They say, *"I feel like I've lost all control!"* I just laugh, and say, *"That means you're headed in the right direction. Keep going! Don't stop now!"* But don't do this in a vacuum. Make sure you set up an effective set of results-focused methods to help everyone see what's going on.

Situations Will Set You Up

Situations arise every day that force us to make decisions that may not be popular. Those "situations" can tend to erode trust and respect if we let them. Every person better know what your motives are when these situations occur, or you're in trouble! Every person must understand that it's situational, not personal.

Beware The Sabotager!

In many organizations is a person known as the sabotager. They have giant egos and lots of passion. They have their own agenda and will do anything to accomplish it. To them, the end justifies the means. In other words, they are willing to do anything necessary to reach their objective. If someone gets in the way, they will do whatever it takes to tear them down. They will discredit, ruin the reputation of, and destroy the person in their way, by whatever means necessary...Typically through manipulation, down right lies, or innuendo. Or, better yet, get someone who's "in their pocket" to do it for them. Or a combination of these. Their greatest skill lies in their ability to totally discredit someone while making themselves look like the innocent victim.

They are masters of manipulation and deceit. They get their power from people who say they "don't want to take sides." (It's *"He said, she said"*, right?) These same people don't want to deal with the conflict, so the sabotager is allowed to continue. The sabotager says things like, *"They just don't like me and they disagree with me so they are blowing this out of proportion. They're out to get me!"* They use lots of subterfuge to mask their true actions and to confuse the issue.

These people will destroy your organization! Those that do the most harm, and are the toughest to catch, are those that are high up in an organization. They hold power over enough people, and can manipulate enough people, that they create a base of people that will support them. I'll say this again, these people will bring your organization to its knees. It will tear you apart!

The weird conundrum behind this is that, what the sabotager is trying to accomplish is not necessarily a bad thing! It's not necessarily "what" they're trying to accomplish, it's "how they're going about it"! It just seems that one of their goals is to tear the organization apart. What they say is, *"Some people won't get it and they have to leave"*! They're right, but they hold this up as a shield to hide behind while they continue to manipulate, lie, and discredit. It seems like they are full of glee as they throw people under the bus – when in reality, they don't have to do it! They could earn trust, build relationships, and take everyone with them if they had a strong desire to do it! They don't need to create chaos. But they do! Is it in their character? Is it impatience, since it takes time to take everyone with you? Do they just not possess good interpersonal skills? Do they really desire to destroy anyone in their path? Do they feel remorse for that, or, for them, is that an acceptable byproduct? Maybe it's a little of each.

The people who try to do something to stop it have no power to do anything. The sabotager has discredited them to a point where those who "don't see it" think that the people trying to stop it "just can't get over it, they don't like him/her, they can't seem to forgive, or they're dwelling on the past". See how good this sabotager is?

So what do you do? The easy answer is to get rid of them! That's also the thing you ought to do. The question really is, "If this person stays, will they change?

And will they change before the organization is destroyed? Do we have the time and resources to deal with it?"

Where Leaders Get It Wrong

Many leaders tell me they've tried the approach I recommend. But when we dig into it, something has always been missed. Usually, it's some person or group that didn't buy in that's responsible for the failure. You must have 100 percent participation. How many people does it take to sink a ship? How many people does it take to tear down trust? One! Don't let anyone slip through the cracks. I've outlined many positive things in this section for leaders to follow. For an opposite view, here's a list of how leaders go wrong. They:
- Allow the 30 percenters to run the organization.
- Fail to organize and muster the 20 percenters.
- Lead by, "do as I say, not as I do".
- Continue to do things that tear down trust.

- Do not lead with integrity.
- Cannot bury or eliminate their ego.
- Are not transparent.
- Allow egos, classes, or ranks to form.
- Disrespect people.
- Don't move fast enough to get rid of "bad apples".
- Give up too soon.
- Simply tell people what to do.
- Don't understand their own behavior style.
- Don't understand other people's behavior style.
- Lack interpersonal skills.
- Completely underestimate or scoff at "culture" as their main job.

You Must Lead!

I know a leader who has told me on several occasions: *"Can't we all just get along? Can't everyone just do their job?"* In that statement is the feeling that everyone must step up. No one can choose your behavior for you – you choose it yourself. I like that. However, it's never that easy. Someone must lead the process. While I've seen people in hourly positions lead the process, it's the exception, not the rule. If you are in a formal leadership position, you, not someone else, must lead it. It won't happen if you don't lead it. You must worry more about the culture or environment than you do with what's going out the back door. If your main focus is on the back door, the 30 percenters will take over. Remember, if you don't lead, someone else surely will. If you aren't leading now, someone surely is! Does that scare you? If it does, you may want to read this book several times! You must build a positive culture and guard it jealously. Don't let anything tear it down!

The Benefits

The benefits of successful leadership and achieving Lean Sustainability include:
- Ownership of the objective.
- A positive culture.
- Contributions from every person.
- An intentional way of thinking.
- Improved results – progress toward being the best.
- Appropriate use of the tools.

Organizations who have achieved these benefits talk about improvements of 20 – 80 percent. Not too shabby for a bunch of touchy-feely stuff, right?

Conclusion

Leaders must empower people if they're serious about becoming the best. They must model the behavior, set clear expectations, and measure results.

Critical concepts learned in this chapter:
1. Never ignore or underestimate a negative culture.
2. Respect every person.
3. Trust is earned.
4. Model the behavior.
5. Work with integrity.
6. Lose the ego.
7. Empower people to achieve outstanding performance.
8. Redefine accountability to include empowerment.
9. Hold yourself accountable first.
10. Deal positively and completely with the Boss from Hell.
11. Make "it" start with you.
12. Blend consistency and flexibility.
13. Don't back off or ease up
14. Take the right people with you.
15. Stop placing blame and get moving.
16. Shift your focus off from yourself and on to the people doing the work.
17. Remember that situations can set you up – it's not personal.
18. Recognize and deal appropriately with the sabotager.

Practice Exercise: Leadership for Sustainability

Complete the following and check your answers with the answer sheet found on page 261. Do not treat this as a test. The goal is not to get a high grade, but to get them all correct. If you don't know an answer, look back through the materials to find it.

1. The definition of empowerment includes creating an _____ in which people want to, and do, take _____ for results.

2. A negative culture can hide _____ unrealized output:
    a. 20 percent.
    b. 100 percent.
    c. Up to 80 percent.
    d. No.

3. The foundation of empowerment is _____.

4. Many leaders ignore or underestimate the impact of:
    a. Donuts at break time.
    b. A negative culture.
    c. The tools of Lean.
    d. Value Stream Mapping.

5. It is difficult if not impossible to measure respect through observing specific behaviors.
    a. True.
    b. False.

6. A leader must _____ the behavior expected of everyone.

7. Your main job as a leader is to:
    a. Remain as the focus of attention.
    b. Take ownership for results.
    c. Hold people accountable for results.
    d. Create the environment.

8. The best way to begin the empowerment process is to begin with great fanfare and celebration and announce all the changes that are coming.
    a. True.
    b. False.

9. Along with imparting their great wisdom and expertise, leaders must learn to _____ by asking _____.

10. A great way to practice respect for others is to treat everyone like an owner or the President of the company.
    a. True.
    b. False.

11. To assist in creating the environment, critique a person's _____ not the decision.

12. The best leaders show respect by respecting you even when you don't _____ it.

13. True accountability begins with:
    a. Involvement, ownership, and keeping score.
    b. Involvement and performance evaluations.
    c. Giving direction, following orders, and punitive measures.
    d. Getting rid of people who mess up.

14. The higher you go in the organization, the _____ the expectations placed on you.
    a. More you can skip.
    b. More you can ignore.
    c. Lower.
    d. Higher.

15. It should start at the top, but it's really effective when everyone _____ together.
    a. Trips up.
    b. Fails.
    c. Learns.
    d. Has lunch.
    e. Bowls.

16. Creating the environment means telling people that you're interested in their ideas and have them submit those ideas to you for review.
    a. True.
    b. False.

17. People need to understand that during hectic times, things get said or done because of the _____, not because it's _____.

18. The possible drawback of complete flexibility and the strength of consistency lies in:
    a. Limited ability to shift people.
    b. Responsibility and ownership of results.
    c. Not using people's skills.
    d. It's easier to manage.
    e. A and C.

19. Given the difficult nature of changing to a sustainable future, you must:
    a. Never give up.
    b. Lead by example.
    c. Take the right people with you.
    d. Outlast the negative people.
    e. All of the above.

20. An effective method of showing respect is to listen without passing judgment.
    a. True.
    b. False.

21. Your focus as a leader, must be on:
    a. Yourself – you're the leader.
    b. The people doing the work.
    c. The 50 percenters.
    d. The Lean team.
    e. A and D.

Leadership for Sustainability

Self Assessment

No				Yes		
1	2	3	4	5	1)	Are we taking any negative culture seriously?
1	2	3	4	5	2)	Do we respect every person?
1	2	3	4	5	3)	Are we earning the trust of every person?
1	2	3	4	5	4)	Do we model the behavior?
1	2	3	4	5	5)	Do we work with integrity?
1	2	3	4	5	6)	Have we lost the ego?
1	2	3	4	5	7)	Am I a leader who empowers?
1	2	3	4	5	8)	Do we use positive accountability?
1	2	3	4	5	9)	Do I hold myself accountable?
1	2	3	4	5	10)	Have we purged the boss(es) from hell?
1	2	3	4	5	11)	Are we leading the Lean process?
1	2	3	4	5	12)	Are we outlasting the negative people?
1	2	3	4	5	13)	Are we blending consistency and flexibility?
1	2	3	4	5	14)	Are we taking the right people with us?
1	2	3	4	5	15)	Have we stopped placing blame?
1	2	3	4	5	16)	Do our people understand that situations can set us up – that it's not personal?
1	2	3	4	5	17)	Have we gotten rid of the sabotagers?

Leadership for Sustainability

Group Discussion Questions

1. Given the self assessment questions on the previous page, what are your organization's:

    a. Strengths:

    b. Weaknesses:

2. What is the impact of ignoring or underestimating a negative culture?

3. How does your organization show respect for every person? Give specific examples:

4. Discuss the methods we use to empower people. What difficulties have you encountered?

5. What difficulties are presented when the management team gives the 30 percenters credibility?

6. On a scale of 1 – 5, with 5 being the highest, what score would you give the leadership in your organization for how they have led the Lean process to date? What changes must be implemented to improve your leadership of the Lean journey?

Practice Exercise Answer Sheet

1. Environment, ownership
2. C
3. Respect
4. B
5. B
6. Model
7. D
8. B
9. Listen, questions
10. A
11. Thought process
12. Deserve
13. A
14. D
15. C
16. B
17. Situation, personal
18. B
19. E
20. A
21. B

Odds and Ends

Everyone has Different Gifts and Talents

We've been saying that everyone must come along on the Lean journey. But I don't want to leave the impression that everyone must be identical in knowledge, skills, and responsibilities. That's impossible because everyone has different gifts and talents. Each person must find their gift or talent and turn it into a skill. This is a very active process. Your gift will not fall out of a tree and hit you on the head! You must pursue it, search for it, and develop it. Ask the question, *"What am I passionate about?"* The answer will lead you in the right direction. Also, you need to turn into skills some things you don't like to do! That's just the way it is! Life will continue. Everyone must do their part – whatever it is!

Some skills required for the Lean journey include the ability to:
- Fabricate.
- Troubleshoot.
- Try things out.
- Test things.
- Design things.
- Tweak processes.
- Take action.
- Organize.
- Lead.
- Manage projects.

- Improve processes.
- Build relationships.
- Listen effectively.
- Speak effectively in groups.
- Write clearly and concisely.
- Implement improvements.
- Solve problems.
- Use Lean tools appropriately and effectively.
- Challenge people.
- Measure and keep score.

Choosing a Trainer or Consultant

Most small organizations do not have a person who can lead the process that I've described. Even if they did, I'm not sure that they would get the respect of every person because most of their fellow associates feel this "chosen" person is part of the current problem. There is too much baggage! I think it's better to look outside the organization. You know the old saying...an expert is someone who drove more than 50 miles. Find someone with skills in every area of the organization. Someone who also understands intimately how the business operates. If you select someone with a technical background, they won't be able to relate to the office, professional, or support staff. Hire someone from an office, professional, or support staff background, and the technical people will chew them up and spit them out. This trainer or consultant must have excellent people skills, technical skills, support department skills, professional staff experience, and financial skills. This is a pretty small window, but the person you choose must be able to gain the trust and respect of every person in the organization. This person must be able to model, teach, and lead both the process and the skills taught in this book.

Do You Need a Lean Champion?

The quick answer to this is yes. But I'd like to discuss it first. The greatest benefit of having a Lean Champion is that you have someone dedicated and focused on Lean activities, projects, and improvements. The huge downside is that once you name a Lean Champion, everyone else flushes their own Lean responsibilities. It's like hiring a cleanup person. Do you want to guarantee that no one cleans up after themselves? Just hire a janitor. Suddenly cleaning is the janitor's job and no one else does it. The same thing can happen when you name a Lean Champion.

My recommendation on this is to begin the Lean training and get everyone moving in the right direction. The Lean Champion will then float to the top at some point. A Lean Champion ideally has the blessing, and has been selected separately, by five groups:
    1. The hourly folks.

2. The management team.
3. Themselves – they must be passionate about it!
4. The support staff.
5. The Lean trainer/consultant.

The Lean Champion must be respected and chosen by all of these people. If one of them disagrees you're looking for trouble. A Lean Champion must possess these skills:

- Great interpersonal skills.
- The ability to build relationships.
- The ability to get things done, no matter the obstacles.
- The guts and savvy not to get run over.
- Technical skills to build or fabricate.
- Process skills to know how things work.
- Computer software skills to create spreadsheets, project plans, and blueprints.
- Able to move among and relate to all levels.
- The ability to manage projects of all difficulties.
- The savvy to know that they can't do everything and the skill to challenge and assist people to implement solutions. In other words, they don't do everything themselves. They must lead the process, not do everything.

It is better to have no Lean Champion at all than have people back off when the Lean Champion is named. It's also better to have no Lean Champion at all then to have the wrong one, or one that's simply the best available option out of several weak choices. The Lean Champion must ensure that every person steps up. They cannot allow people to dump all Lean activities because they think it's the Lean Champion's job. It's not. It's everyone's.

Do You Need a Lean Team?

I'm not sure on this one. The huge disadvantage is that with a team, it's worse than one person. If a Lean Champion causes everyone to flush their Lean responsibilities, think what a Lean team will cause. Pretty soon the Lean team is the only group doing Lean. My recommendation is that the Lean team should be a cross functional group made up of people from every level and function, who report directly to the president or owner. Almost like a board of directors, they have no responsibilities as an advisory group other than to advise (this responsibility is over and above their regular job, of course). They must be very respected by their peers, professional in their actions, and listened to by the president or owner.

Remember, it is better to have no Lean team at all than to have the rest of the organization flush their Lean responsibilities when the team is named.

What are the Characteristics of a Sustained Lean Process?

- Every person is respected.
- Every person is actively involved.
- A positive culture is created and guarded jealously.
- Every job or position is involved.
- People think in a new way.
- People "get it".
- Results are measured, visual, and improved.
- Appropriate tools are used for the situation.
- People get things done. There is a bias for action.
- Leaders empower – they create the environment in which people want to, and do take ownership for results.
- Leaders lead with integrity. They respect people and earn the trust of every person in the organization.
- Every person owns the objective.

Why do Organizations Fail to Sustain Lean?

- They rely on a Lean Champion or Lean team.
- They permit a negative culture.
- They let people slide.
- They demand compliance, not ownership.
- They focus only on the tools of Lean.

- They don't understand how to truly sustain Lean.
- They think that people won't change.
- They want a quick fix.
- They think a technical solution, or engineering approach is the only way to do Lean.
- They listen to Lean gurus who have success in specific limited situations and who can't relate to every department.
- They listen to Lean gurus who previously worked in a company with a great culture which they underestimate when they try to help someone else.
- They follow a trainer or consultant who only knows and teaches the tools.
- They follow a trainer or consultant who won't deal with the negative people. They say, "*That's your job! I only deal with Lean!*"

Sequence of Events

Here is what I see as the sequence of events in your Lean journey. Some of these are one time events and some reoccur at regular intervals.

Step 1: Involve everyone in several hours of Lean culture training to "experience" Lean in a positive way. This training is the foundation to Lean sustainability and must focus on moving people in a positive direction. The goal of this training is to both educate and to put people in a position to "choose" to come along. They must "experience" the subject, not just be told about it!

Helpful hint: File the Power Point presentation – it doesn't work!

Step 2: Involve everyone in 5S training to learn a basic Lean tool and begin the hands-on portion of the process. Every person must get involved by completing a project connected with their job. (Each person must always have a project that they are working on in addition to their daily work).

Step 3: Create Lean event project teams to begin applying basic Lean techniques to critical processes.

Step 4: Create a Lean advisory board, and select a Lean Champion. (Do not allow people in the organization to back off when this step is implemented).

Note: This step is optional.

Step 5: Receive advanced Lean tool training (for specific people) to further refine and improve processes.

Step 6: Apply advanced Lean tools to critical processes.

Step 7: Continue training for all associates on various additional Lean or related subjects for all associates on a recurring schedule to inject energy and enthusiasm.

Step 8: Lean advisory board assesses progress, and suggests improvements.

How to Get Traction

Getting traction means getting everyone moving toward Lean implementation and sustainability. Here are some ideas:

1. Everyone picks a project in their area and implements it. If 50 people implement a project every three months, you will have 200 implemented improvements in one year!

2. Create a supplier/customer/family open house to be held six months in the future. The first day is for suppliers, customers, and other business guests. This is typically held on Friday.

Then, on Saturday have a big, blow out, picnic open house for employees, families, and friends. This gives you six months to get the building and grounds in shape. Sometimes you need an event that gives you a target date to get things done.

Junior High Behavior

Something interesting happens when I do Lean training. The 30 percenters will make it unpopular to think the training is a good thing. Their attitude is like a junior high student that scoffs at anyone trying to learn, or even listen. My advice? Ignore them. Just continue to learn and get involved. You're going to win in the end, so don't worry about it.

The Stages of Lean Implementation

- Initial excitement — Maybe things will finally change.
- Reality sets in — Hey, this isn't happening like we thought, why isn't it changing?
- Ownership — Waiting for others to act isn't getting us anywhere – I need to stop pointing fingers and get to work.
- Floaters are identified (those that don't "get it" float to the top) — The 50 and 30 percenters lose their power and either convert or become unemployable.
- Traction is gained — The organization begins to implement dozens of improvements leading to 25 – 50% capacity gain.

Have You Discovered the Missing Piece of the Puzzle?

So, what's your missing piece? Or, are there several missing pieces to your puzzle? Are you frustrated with your progress? Are you achieving the results you not only want, but need, in order to become, or stay, more competitive?

If you are not where you want to be, or need to be, I would challenge you, first of all, to take everyone in a formal leadership role through this book. Use the brown bag lunch process I described up front. Use it to identify the missing pieces and develop goals, strategies, and action plans to make the changes you require. From there, engage your entire organization in this process of positive change.

There are no excuses for putting this off. You hold the key to the missing piece of the puzzle for your organization. There can be, and are, no excuses for not beginning this process today. If not you, who? If not now, when?

Reference Bibliography

20-50-30- Rule: While I experienced this situation myself, I later learned the numbers breakdown through Price Pritchett. "Resistance. Moving Beyond The Barriers to Change. A Handbook For People Who Make Things Happen". Price Pritchett, 1996.

The Lean Office: Productivity Press. "The Lean Office Collected Practices and Cases". New York, 2005.

Cover illustration: Fotolia.com. Final Piece Series (copyright) James Steidl #1728451.

Index

-Numbers-
5S 180
– Set in Order 183
– Shine 184
– Sort 181
– Standardize 187
– Sustain 188
5W's and an H 211
20-50-30 Rule Applied to Technical Skills . . 123

-A-
Accountability Starts at the Top 236
Additional Thoughts 155
Anticipate What Can Happen 131

-B-
Barrier 38
Be a Professional 121
Be Like the Maytag Repairman 131
Beware The Sabotager? 247
Blur the Lines 93
Breeding Ground for 30 Percenters . . . 129
Bribery Works 118
Boss from Hell 239
Build a House with a Hammer? 174

-C-
Changing Habits 129
Choosing a Trainer or Consultant . . . 265
Conclusion: Law #1 50
Conclusion: Law #2 77
Conclusion: Law #3 98
Conclusion: Law #4 134
Conclusion: Law #5 165
Conclusion: Law #6 214
Conclusion: Leadership for Sustainability . . 252
Consistency vs. Flexibility 242
Continue to Learn 121
Creating Desire 42
Culture Change 62

-D-

Dancing to the Oldies .	176
Definition of Lean	18
Desire	40
Do You Need a Lean Champion? .	266
Do You Need a Lean Team? .	268
Don't' Back Off or Ease Up .	243

-E-

Elevate your Constraint	122
Every Person must Change .	107
Everyone has Different Gifts and Talents	264

-F-

Five S	180
– Set in Order	183
– Shine	184
– Sort	181
– Standardize	187
– Sustain	188
Five W's and an H	211

-G-

Getting Things Done Takes Horsepower	117
Getting Traction .	130
Good Judgment .	128
Greatest Obstacles	148
Grow People Who "Get It"	237
Guy Called "They" Doesn't Exist .	133

-H-

Have You Discovered the Missing Piece of the Puzzle?	275
Helpful Hints on Creating a Scoreboard	160
How to Get Traction	272
How We Get it Wrong .	30

-I-

It Must Start at The Top?	240
It Takes Horsepower .	96

-J-
Junior High Behavior 273

-K-
Kaizen 190
   - Event: Benefits and Drawbacks . . . 191
Kanban 204
   - What is Kanban 204
   - Goals 205
   - Action Plans to Create a Kanban System . 205
Key People May Resist 96

-L-
Law #1: Group Discussion Questions . . . 56
Law #1: Lean Requires that You take Everyone . 24, 36
Law #1: Self Assessment 55
Law #2: Group Discussion Questions . . . 85
Law #2: Lean is a Culture 25, 60
Law #2: Self Assessment 84
Law #3: Group Discussion Questions . . . 103
Law #3: Lean Must Encompass Every Area . . 26, 88
Law #3: Self Assessment 102
Law #4: Group Discussion Questions . . . 141
Law #4: Lean is a Way of Thinking . . . 27, 106
Law #4: Self Assessment 140
Law #5: Group Discussion Questions . . . 170
Law #5: Lean Focuses on Results, Not Activities . 28, 144
Law #5: Self Assessment 170
Law #6: Group Discussion Questions . . . 221
Law #6: Self Assessment 220
Law #6: Lean is a Set of Tools, or Methods, for Finding
      and Eliminating Waste 29, 174
Leadership Benefits 252
Leadership for Sustainability 224
Lean Metrics and Empowerment 145
Lean Metrics Defined 144
Lean Sustainability Group Discussion Questions . 260
Lean Sustainability Self Assessment . . . 259
Lean Tools 178
Learn to See Waste 111
Learn to Think Differently 110

Got Lean? Index

-M-

Maintenance People Must Change Their Mindset	130
Marketing vs. Selling	128
Measurement, Start to Finish	154
Mistake #1	88
Mistake #2	89
Mix Them Up	95

-O-

Outrun the "Foot"	133
Overcome the Obstacles	115
Ownership	47

-P-

Pareto Analysis	207
Patience, Control and Chaos	109
People must be Self-Managed	124
People, Process, and Technology	239
Perfect Attendance	93
Practice Exercise Answer Sheet: Law #1	57
Practice Exercise Answer Sheet: Law #2	86
Practice Exercise Answer Sheet: Law #3	104
Practice Exercise Answer Sheet: Law #4	142
Practice Exercise Answer Sheet: Law #5	172
Practice Exercise Answer Sheet: Law #6	222
Practice Exercise Answer Sheet: Leadership	261
Practice Exercise: Law #1	52
Practice Exercise: Law #2	80
Practice Exercise: Law #3	99
Practice Exercise: Law #4	136
Practice Exercise: Law #5	167
Practice Exercise: Law #6	215
Practice Exercise: Leadership for Sustainability	254
Process Fixation	159
Products Available	285

-S-

Scoreboard Obstacles	150
Sequence of Events	270
Services Available	286
Set Goals	156
Setup Time Reduction – What's it Worth?	195

Got Lean?   Index

Situations Will Set You Up	247
Six Laws of Lean	22
SMED – Single Minute Exchange of Dies	195
Stages of Lean Implementation	274
Start Simply	175
Stop Doing it and See if Anyone Notices	129
Stop Placing Blame and Get Moving	245
Suggestion Systems Get You in Trouble	119

-T-

Take the Right People with You	244
Technical Approach vs. People Approach	132
Theoretically Perfect Goal: Law #1	39
Theoretically Perfect Goal: Law #2	61
Theoretically Perfect Goal: Law #3	92
Theoretically Perfect Goal: Law #4	106
Theoretically Perfect Goal: Law #5	144
Theoretically Perfect Goal: Law #6	174
Theoretically Perfect Goals	114
Think "Perfect", not "Good enough"	130
Think Process not People	132
Thinking in a New Way	108
Tool Matrix	179
Total Productive Maintenance (TPM)	199
- Definition	199
- Goals	199
- Critical Factors	200
- Responsibilities within TPM	202

-V-

Value Stream Mapping	193

-W-

Want to Improve? You Gotta Keep Score!	153
We Can't Change Time, But We Can Change How We Use It.	122
We Must Work Together	95
What are the Characteristics of a Sustained Lean Process?	269
Where is Your Focus?	246
Where Leaders Get It Wrong	250
Why Do Organizations Fail to Sustain Lean?	269

Got Lean?   Index

Why the Need to Change   107
Why We Fail   177

-Y-
You Must Lead!   251

About the Author

Randy Lubbers is the owner of Lubbers & Associates, a consulting firm dedicated to providing highly effective training and consulting at a reasonable cost. He has been in business for over 16 years and has consulted with dozens of organizations. Randy has trained thousands of people in problem solving, Lean methods, leadership, and various other subjects. He was born, raised, and lives in West Michigan.

Randy has been in and around successful organizations for more than 34 years. He uses his experience to assist others in learning what it really takes to be productive and successful. He creates his own materials and presents them in a practical, hands-on way.

Randy's primary focus in any consulting situation or training session is making a connection with each person. He feels that earning the trust and respect of each person is essential for an effective learning environment. With his unique blend of knowledge and skills, Randy can relate to any person in an organization, from front to back. He uses all of his experiences to accomplish this, including those as a Journeyman Eyelet Tool & Die Maker, supervisor, plant manager, and currently as a business owner with interest in several businesses.

Randy's passion is to assist people in transforming their own behavior and the culture of their organization, so that they can become the best at what they do. His training sessions have impacted many lives and while he always creates his own materials, this is his first book. It is an outgrowth of his passion to assist others and is based on his unique insights gained over many years of assisting many different types of organizations. His client list includes dozens of both small and mid-size organizations.

Got Lean? Other Products and Services

| **Products Available from Lubbers & Associates:** |

- Got Lean? Discovering the Missing Piece of the Puzzle - $29.95.

- Got Pareto? Using Pareto Analysis to Focus and Prioritize. (A workbook) - $19.95.

- Got 5S? Using 5S to Implement Lean - $19.95.

- Got CQI? A Step-by-step Guide to Obtaining CQI Certification - $75.00.

- The Trilogy:

    (1) Got It? A Handbook for Developing People who "Get It".

    Coming soon!

    (2) Got Leadership? Developing Leaders who Allow People to Act.

    (3) Got Success? A Field Guide to Achieving Greatness.

- Who Moved the Water Cooler? Creating a Suggestion System that Actually Works. *Coming soon!*

To order any of our available products:
- Call or fax – (269)751-7077
- E-mail: rlubbers@juno.com
- Website: www.lubbersandassociates.com

Quantity discounts are available upon request.

Check out our complete line of products and services on our website at www.lubbersandassociates.com.

Services Available from Lubbers & Associates:

General Programs:
- ❑ DISC Personal Profile System
- ❑ Team Building
- ❑ Employee Involvement
- ❑ Train-the-Trainer
- ❑ Supervisory Training/Empowerment
- ❑ Interpersonal Communications
- ❑ Conflict Resolution
- ❑ Time Management
- ❑ Basic Project Management
- ❑ Lean Metrics
- ❑ Finance for Non-Financial Managers
- ❑ Facilitator Training
- ❑ Business Planning and Development
- ❑ Team Leadership
- ❑ Leadership
- ❑ Leading Effective Meetings
- ❑ Effective Coaching
- ❑ Basic Budgeting

Technical/Process Programs:
- ❑ Lean Strategies: Culture, 5S, SMED, Value Stream Mapping, various other Lean Tools and Applications
- ❑ Problem Solving (Basic, Advanced, Facilitation, and 8D)
- ❑ Statistical Process Control (SPC)
- ❑ Basic Geometric Dimensioning and Tolerancing (GD&T)
- ❑ Basic, Intermediate, and Advanced Math
- ❑ Blueprint Reading
- ❑ FMEA
- ❑ Certified Quality Inspectors
- ❑ Jobs Skills Training – Development and Delivery
- ❑ Basic Measuring Tools
- ❑ Troubleshooting
- ❑ Various Safety Program

Check out our complete line of products and services on our website at www.lubbersandassociates.com.

Call Me if You Need Help

If you are frustrated with your progress toward Lean implementation, or just beginning, I invite you to contact me. I've honed and refined my process over 34 years in and around business. It is unique, deliberate, focused, systematic, and people centered. It creates energy and enthusiasm for the people who attend. It works! Tired of the old methods? Then do something different! Call me today! Your organization will never be the same!

Phase One - Lean Culture:
People learn to step up to get things done. People choose to own the Lean process and willingly embrace it.

Phase Two – Lean 5S:
People turn theory and concepts into action. Changes begin to be seen in every area. Sights are set on 25-50% improvement in capacity.

Phase Three - Lean Events (Value Stream Mapping, SMED, Pull Systems/Kanban, etc.):
Specific focus areas are chosen for improvement. Specific tools are taught and used to directly improve the targeted process. Several events are implemented back to back using any one of the above tools as appropriate.

To contact us:
- Call or fax – (269)751-7077
- E-mail: rlubbers@juno.com
- Website: www.lubbersandassociates.com

Here's What People are Saying

- "Randy brings a very strong experience-based approach to the Lean training."
- "Randy does a great job of keeping everyone active and interested."
- "He made me aware of how the industry is struggling and also how making improvements is so easy."
- "Randy taught Lean training in a very interesting and creative way. I was challenged."
- "Randy was very knowledgeable and passes that knowledge on to the listeners."
- "I thought the class was very good with realistic suggestions for improvement in the real world."
- "He helped us establish the basis and fundamentals for our Lean journey."
- "Randy teaches in a way that you don't realize you're learning until you see how you've made it work everyday."